Free Us For Joyful Obedience

A Primer on Pastoral Caregiving From a Pastor's Heart

Monty Brown

Bloomington, IN Milton Keynes, UK

authorHOUSE®

AuthorHouse™
1663 Liberty Drive, Suite 200
Bloomington, IN 47403
www.authorhouse.com
Phone: 1-800-839-8640

AuthorHouse™ *UK Ltd.*
500 Avebury Boulevard
Central Milton Keynes, MK9 2BE
www.authorhouse.co.uk
Phone: 08001974150

This book is a work of non-fiction. Unless otherwise noted, the author and the publisher make no explicit guarantees as to the accuracy of the information contained in this book and in some cases, names of people and places have been altered to protect their privacy.

First published by AuthorHouse 12/5/2006

ISBN: 978-1-4259-8012-2 (sc)
ISBN: 978-1-4259-8769-5 (e)

Library of Congress Control Number: 2006910335

Printed in the United States of America
Bloomington, Indiana

This book is printed on acid-free paper.

This book is dedicated to my high school sweetheart Jane, who still loves and excites me, and keeps me young and crazy after all these years.

ACKNOWLEDGEMENTS

Paul Smith articulated the 3 Rules of Effective Pastoral Ministry. *Frank Shaffer* and *Paul Stadelman* showed me how that looks as a day-in-day-out, year after year, life.

Norman Redlich enunciated the rule that if we do the right thing, it will somehow, always, (even when we can't see it then) turn out to be the most strategic thing. *Emerson Wood* and *Tom Dunlap* showed me how that gets lived out.

Michael Ognibene (who rests comfortably on the breast of Jesus) and *Vaughn Michael* showed me how the mystical mirror of Jesus works (without ever using that term) in the honesty of their living and their counsel.

Joe and Betsy Brown gave their best to raise me to know love as a daily staple. *Josh and Bethany Brown* continue giving me reminders of how proud and blessed I am to be their father.

My covenant discipleship group for the past twelve years (the *Holy Club: Tim Allen, Michael Estep, Sara Lamb, Jim Reed, Paul Russell,* and *Bart Thompson*) has given me a safe place to confess, the wisdom to keep me closer to being on course, and the good humor to remind me of the fourth rule of effective ministry.

Jane Brown and *Lynn Henson* gave countless hours to proofreading, editing, and encouraging. The *Flock of Saint Marks UMC* both remind me what the *Body of Christ* looks like and inspire me to remember what a blessed calling is that of a pastor. They made publication of this book possible.

TABLE OF CONTENTS

INTRODUCTION

This book was written in response to a call asking me to teach the Pastoral Care component of the West Virginia Annual Conference Pastoral Ministry Licensing School. It was originally designed to be an entry level instructional book for that purpose, but has come to take on some other functions.

It is designed for those who are answering for the first time the call to pastoral ministry *and* for a renewal of the passion for that calling in those who have been doing it for so long, that they may have allowed themselves to forget what that calling is all about. It also is instructional for lay folks who are training to enter into partnership with their pastor to assist in the provision of pastoral caregiving – in hospitals, homes, and nursing homes.

While it is a "nuts and bolts" practical "how-to" book, it also explores some of the theology that underlies those techniques – why we do it the way we do. "Doing theology" seems intimidating to some folks, as a very high brow academic study that can only be undertaken at a graduate school level. I disagree. My colleague Paul Rebelo tells me that I practice "folk theology," and I think he is right. The contents here are not written as the theology of the academy, which often needs to be translated before it can be applied into the pew, hospital, and spiritual counselor's office (confessional.) Instead, it focuses on the "story" component of the nexus between scripture and daily living.

In sum, it is an introduction to pastoral caregiving that *arises from* the heart, and is *lived out of* the heart. Jesus said that we are indeed to love the Lord our God with all of our heart, soul, mind, and strength. And surely He is correct in describing how pastoral care is a reflection of that love toward our neighbor as ourself – it requires deep concentration and application from all four of these God given faculties. It is hoped that the "heart knowledge" in this book will bear fruit in all four of these vessels of God's grace in our lives, since we love in response to the grace that is given us.

This "book document" is but a reflection of, and upon, my "human document" – the pages of which are covered with the fingerprints of so many saints, and so many life experiences, which have shaped me and my approach to pastoral caregiving.

As such, the reader must be forewarned that this little book is not THE resource for pastoral caregiving. It is designed to be an entry level primer, and is really only about what has worked for me and the flocks entrusted to my care. It clearly is the product of who I am, what I believe, and the roads that I have traveled. The reader, therefore, deserves to be alerted to the background, and the accompanying baggage and prejudices that I bring to the table. A few pertinent details follow:

I haven't always been a pastor. I graduated with an undergraduate degree in Bible and Religion, originally intending to answer a call to pastoral ministry. Then, one summer during college, after working as a staff member in my home church, my twenty-something year old naiveté had a hard time coping with the "politics" of the church. I reasoned that my religion was too important to me to mess it up by getting my paycheck from the church, so I ventured into what I thought would be another form of ministry – the practice of law.

Following the mandatory three years of law school and being admitted to the bar, I was actively engaged in the practice of law, with the primary focus being on trial practice. I was in private practice for three years (doing a lot of criminal defense work) and then was in public practice for twelve years (as a Prosecuting Attorney.) Lest the irony of that latter "twist" go unnoticed, I realized (finally) what a sense of humor God has in allowing me to use pugilistic nature of "church politics" as an escape from the church, and then in allowing me to plunge headlong into secular politics, where I found that the gloves really come off. Following my defeat for my third term as the elected Prosecuting Attorney, my beloved wife told me that she knew what I must surely know – namely, that I belonged in seminary to prepare for the practice of pastoral ministry.

The twists and turns of my human document could perhaps be fleshed out in more detail in a different little book, but suffice it to say here that I have been over and again amazed at how the experiences of my "first career" have borne fruit in answering (finally) what "may" have been my first calling – that of pastoral ministry.

Often, I have heard people say, "Wow! That's quite a switch. How have you made the transition?" It has not been quite so different in many respects. Many of the people skills are much the same. And, given that I looked upon my whole career in the law as a form of ministry, the mindset is not so much different either. (The Dean of NYU Law School told us on the first day of orientation that there were two groups of students gathered before him: (1) those who want to do good, and (2) those who want to do well. It was an apt description, but I have been blessed on occasion to witness those who were able to do both.)

Two overriding insights that come to me from the transition, and which do indeed shape my view of pastoral caregiving, are:

(1)   While I was formerly in the business of making people pay for mistakes they had made, now my calling is to be a vehicle for the dispensation of God's Grace and Forgiveness to people who have made mistakes.

(2)   I have also come to understand in my own life, and thus have been able to see it perhaps more easily in others, that God's Resurrection Power is about redemption. There are no life circumstances which, when turned over to God, cannot be redeemed and made to serve a good and useful purpose in God's Kingdom.

Aside from not having been subjected to the horrors of the battlefield or a prison camp, there's not a whole lot that I can experience in life that can shock me. My past has served me well in that respect. I have been able to relate from my personal experience to many things that a "first career pastor" has only experienced through being well read, or vicariously through the experiences of the members of her flock.

Throughout my whole adult lifetime, I have been very active in the Church, and have come to see much of what goes on in the halls of church governance as well as in the private lives of pastors and their families. Being an active layperson actually gave me invitation into some parsonage family situations that pastors would not be willing to share with professional colleagues. I have seen much of the good that the Church does, as well as some of the carnage and long lasting wounds that get inflicted – mostly accidentally – by people who are quite certain of the rightness of their thinking and their conduct.

All of this, along with being a student of the history of the Church, has admittedly shaped me with a penchant toward the importance of *humility*. How strongly we believe we are right about something is no guarantee of how right we indeed are. Christian warriors on a quest can indeed be very, very dangerous – to both the Church as an institution and to the Church as the *Body of Christ*, which indeed is our calling.

I was, through no choice of my own, brought up as a Christian of the Methodist (later United Methodist) denomination. Although I have attempted herein to be non-denominational in my approach, I must admit that who I am and the *bent* that I have for pastoral caregiving is shaped by that denominational affiliation. This will be reflected in certain (few! I promise) references to our polity (*United Methodist Discipline*) but even more so to a particular distinctive quality of our denomination, which we call *Doing the Theological Task*.

Doing the Theological Task means that we are a Church that really believes the dictum of John Wesley: *In essentials, unity; in non-essentials, liberty; and in all things, love.*[1] This means that we have fewer dogma that mandate unanimity of mind among our members. As one person put it, *"United Methodists are not only allowed to think; they are required to do so."*

This is at least a two edged sword in pastoral caregiving. It gives more freedom for people to *work out their own salvation*, but also comes with the accompanying scripturally grounded consequence: *with fear and trembling.* (Philippians 2:12) Issues of the soul (of which the pastoral caregiver is the doctor) are not fixed with a quick reference to dogma which the patient can simply take as a pill, and call back in the morning.

I say "at least" a two edged sword, because it also (when misapplied) can put too heavy an emphasis on *thinking.* And when the Doctor of the Soul is called into intensive practice, it is often when a crisis has erupted, for which *mere thinking* rarely provides the needed cure/growth. The language of the heart and the affairs of the emotions are rarely fully addressed by mere rational thought or language (with possible exceptions being the language of poetry, music, and silence – but none of these are "rational thought language.")

These are some of the pieces of baggage that my human document brings to this book document. If they are radically different from your perspective, it is my hope that you will, nonetheless, be able to redeem something of value from that which follows. But I was obligated to lay it out clearly here at the beginning, so you can perhaps better understand some of what has led me to see experiences as I have.

The Feast of All Saints, 2006
Saint Marks United Methodist Church
Charleston, West Virginia

---

1   Wesley's eighteenth century language used the word "charity" rather than love, and has been modified here in much the same way "charity" in the King James Version of the Bible (in use in the Rev'd Mr. Wesley's day) of 1 Corinthians 13 has been modified to the contemporary expression of that same concept: "love."

I also note that the same concept is not unique to the people called Methodist. Pope John XXIII said as much: *"In essentials, unity; in doubtful matters, liberty; in all things charity."* (*Ad Petri Cathedram*)

"Each of our lives is a human document."

Vaughn Michael, Jr.

Holy God of ancient glory,
Choosing man and woman, too;
Abr'am's faith and Sarah's story
Formed a people bound to you.
Alleluia, Alleluia,
To your covenant keep us true.

> Covenant, new again in Jesus,
> Star child born to set us free;
> Sent to heal us, sent to teach us
> How love's children we might be.
> Alleluia, Alleluia,
> Risen Christ, our Savior he!

Lift we then our human voices,
In the songs that faith would bring
Live we then in human choices
Lives that, like our music, sing:
Alleluia, Alleluia,
Joined in love our praises ring!

Bishop William Boyd Grove
United Methodist Hymnal, #100

Each of our lives is a human document ... meant by God to sing!

1

I AM CALLED TO BE A PASTOR

*Enable us, O God, to do all things
as unto You; that small things may
be filled with greatness, and great
things may be crowned with humility; through Jesus Christ, our Lord.
AMEN.*

"I am called to be a pastor."

So many of us remember that call, are diligent to stay
in touch with the One Who made the call (so as to discern
its daily refinements) and still give thanks each day for that
call.

However, what that call to being a pastor means is not
the same for each one who has responded, "Here I am,
Lord. Send me."

Just before I left home and job to go to seminary, my
pastor and his pastor spouse took my wife and me out to a
farewell dinner. I asked both of them, "What's the best part
of being a pastor?" Although their language was individualized, they both answered alike:

The best part of being a pastor is how people
– sometimes, even people who don't know you at
all – open up their lives down to an intimate level,

3

and invite you in. Invite you in to share some of the most intense and important times in their life.

It would be some time later, during seminary, when I would be introduced to the concept of **the Vicar of Christ**. I learned it in a sacramental context:

> Oh, what a shame that Jesus Himself is not here to be the Celebrant for Holy Communion, but He sent His Vicar as a stand-in, as a suitable substitute. And that is sufficient, for He Himself will appear in the elements ("in a spiritual sense" we United Methodists are careful to add.)

A "sufficient substitute" in a holy sacrament. And a "sufficient substitute" in providing pastoral care.

Perhaps I came to realize this most in the hospital pastoral care setting. Both during my CPE (clinical pastoral education) settings and during years spent as a volunteer "night pastor on call," in a local hospital, I was constantly thrust into situations of intensity with people who didn't know me at all.

But, because I wore the collar (the hospital chaplain ID badge, or whatever other identification was in place) they said (always silently and almost certainly mostly unconsciously) "Right now, in this overwhelming situation, I need Jesus. What a shame I can't see Him with my eyes, but He sent His Vicar. And this is sufficient. This one I can trust. This one I can bare myself unto."

Because I work within a polity of submissive itinerancy, I stay and move in each local church setting, at the call of the Bishop. In each appointment (at times of both my coming and my going, and at many times in between) I am wont to often say:

> Pastors are like spark plugs: (1) The spark never originates in them; they are only to be conductors of that spark from God; and (2) Thread one out and thread another one in, and the engine (Church) keeps right on running.

When someone is in need of pastoral care, they are in a life situation where the divine spark planted by the Creator within them hungers and longs and needs to touch the

Source of that spark – the Holy One Who made, loves, sustains, and enlivens them. Jesus is God enfleshed, and they need to touch Jesus. What a shame Jesus ascended unto the right hand of God and is no longer physically present, as He was in first century Palestine. Ah, but He sent His Vicar, and that is sufficient.

It is an awesome calling – to be Jesus' stand-in – the Vicar of Christ. And we do it best when we get ourselves out of the way as much as possible and let Jesus flow through us. We do it best when we model for the Church "being the Body of Christ" in a wounded, hurting world.

And it is indeed an awesome responsibility – this calling.

Being called into ministry is wonderful – for both clergy and laity. It is certainly not a "one size fits all.

For too long in my ministry, I allowed myself to feel diminished in importance and worth by the descriptions spoken by those who seemed to be "front and center" among the clergy: "Oh, she/he is *[just]* a chaplain of that church."

The word "just" was sometimes said aloud, was sometimes merely implied, and was sometimes (I now realize) never intended, but heard by the ear of my own insecurities.

As my times in pastoral ministry rolled along, I began to realize:

- The average shelf life is about three years for each new and wonderful "greatest thing in the life of the Church since the Great Awakening of the 19th century" (etc.)
- The (not always) subtle message that pastors hear so often (that they begin to think is actually their calling) is that we need to "fix" this church.
- The folks who sit in the pews are, largely, tired of being constantly tinkered with by ecclesiastical plumbers and mechanics like they are some kind of machinery or laboratory mice.
- More than anything else, the folks who sit in the pews want *and need* a pastor who loves them, and who is there walking beside them as

> a Friend, a suitable substitute *in body* for their
> very best friend, Jesus.

Two very short vignettes opened before me one week to help my eyes see myself no longer as "just" a chaplain to a church.

I was visiting a pastor friend near the end of his first year in an appointment. He is a very gifted pastor and has a reputation as an effective pastor. I asked him how the first year was coming to a close.

He expressed great frustration. He told me that the flock, under the leadership of the former long term pastor, had developed some bad habits. The former pastor had deeply loved the flock, and was deeply loved by them. But the former pastor had not been a good program leader. And now, my pastor friend told me, the members had grown "lazy," and "almost impossible" to motivate into the action and activities that this new pastor envisioned for them.

Second vignette: The following Sunday, as part of my church's "Homecoming" a former pastor, now retired, was invited to return to preach. Later, at the church picnic, the retired pastor and I had a few private moments.

He told me,

> "You know I spent most of my ministry being a cheerleader, an administrator, a motivator, and a trainer – always trying to get the people on board with this program or that program. But since I have retired, and had opportunities like today to revisit churches, I've found that what really mattered, what really stuck with, and what really made a difference in their relationship with God, were the times when they needed a pastor.
>
> "When they needed a pastor to tend to their wounds, to hear them out, to accompany them through struggles, and to be real and honest with them. When they needed me to love them.
>
> "Ah, those programs were all good, I suppose. But they didn't really make the impact on their lives – or, for that matter, on the Kingdom [of God] – nearly so much as when I was being a good pastor.

"It's difficult to see that in the moment. The allure and excitement of each new program is powerful. But, if I had it to do over, I'd do it a lot differently."

Oh, don't get me wrong; the visions and programs of an effective church are important and meaningful. And they can help us remember our calling to reach out in loving ministry to others, and to not just focus on our own needs.

We love, because God first loved us.
(1 John 4:7,11)

With each person, this is the starting point and the daily centering point to know -- *in head **and in heart** –* that they are indeed a **beloved child of God, precious and beautiful to behold**.

Otherwise, all the "do good" programs of the Church are things to do out of a sense of guilt, out of an inability to say no to a persuasive leader, and / or another feather in the cap on the head of either the work righteousness disciple or the self-interested praise seeker.

Somewhere from within that deep reservoir from which preachers draw illustrations, but (in derogation of those rules learned in seminary, to always footnote our sources) for which origins are so often forgotten, I encountered a story about a seriously wounded soldier on the battlefield being ministered to by a chaplain:

"Do you know Jesus as your Lord and Savior, son?"

"Reverend, I can't really talk about that now. I'm too cold to even be able to think."

The chaplain removed his own coat and wrapped it around the wounded man. "Would you like for me to pray with you, son?"

"No, chaplain. My throat is too parched to be able to pray. I am just so very, very thirsty."

The battlefield pastoral caregiver lifted his own canteen to the man's lips and let him drink as much as he wanted. Before he could ask the soldier a third time, the wounded man said,

"Now, pastor, please pray for me. Pray to the
One who causes you to be so kind."

Just a story. Just a sermon illustration from some un-remembered source. Fact or not, I don't know. But it is true. It is as true as the historical fact of Chaplain Owens,[2] who left his pastoral appointment in a church to volunteer as a military chaplain in the Pacific Theatre of Operation during World War II. The war took too great a toll on him to ever be able to return to a church pulpit. But of the 500+ soldiers he baptized, 81 went on to become ordained pastors.

"I am called to be a pastor."

Some folks might think I am "*just*" a chaplain to my church.

I do my "chaplain" work in private, intimate, intensive situations – that never get reports, never get attention.

They're just little moments during intensive times when – if I get myself out of the way enough – pastoral care re-ceiver and giver are embraced by the strong loving arms of God.

> *Enable us, O God, to do all things as unto You; that small things may be filled with greatness, and great things may be crowned with humil-ity; through Jesus Christ, our Lord. AMEN.*

---

[2] The uncle of a parishioner in a church I once served

8

A Nugget

THAT LICENSE TO PREACH
(ORDINATION CERTIFICATE, ETC.)
AND 99¢ ENTITLES YOU TO A CUP OF COFFEE
FROM THE LOCAL FAST FOOD RESTAURANT.

IT DOES NOT ENTITLE YOU TO BUTT IN.

One of the things I learned early – prior to answering the call to pastoral ministry – as a layperson, is that too many pastors think they have the right to butt in to anyone's life that they think they could "fix."

Don't.

Stay out, unless you are invited.

People need to want to change, need to want your help, before you will do much good.

None of your training entitles you to run other people's lives. All of your training and life's experiences, at best, equip you to be a spiritual friend, a Doctor of the Soul. Learn from the medical doctors; they only treat when they are asked. Indeed, it is a violation of their ethics to charge in and treat someone who doesn't want it (absent a court order.)

Whenever you get the urge to Butt In,

STOP

ASK YOURSELF: Whose needs am I really trying to serve here – theirs or mine?

The answer may help you understand yourself better.

Look to Jesus' example. Before He healed, He asked, "Do you want to be made well?"

You're not better than Jesus.

Don't butt in.

Stay out, unless you are invited.

(Even when other folks in the Church want you to butt in … especially then!)

9

2
WHAT DIFFERENCE DOES IT MAKE IN YOUR MINISTRY?

Our deepest center is God's most precious gift to each of us, and so there is no way it can exist on its own. Our deepest, truest center is relational: it is our identity in Christ, daily developing and urging us forth in a whole way of living and choosing for others.

George Aschenbrenner[3]

So you think you are called to be a pastoral caregiver. What does that mean?

Although I am loathe to allow the practice of pastoral ministry to be dissected in the same way that our culture has handled almost every other profession (we are indeed one of the last "general practitioners" in existence in 21st century America) I must recognize the Apostle Paul's wisdom that different people are given different gifts for different tasks.

---

[3]   In article, "A Hidden Self Grown Strong," appearing in the excellent compendium that is *an absolute must* for any pastor serious about doing spiritual direction: Robert J. Wicks, ed., *Handbook of Spirituality for Ministers* (New York: Paulist Preess, 1995)

11

Although all pastoral ministers are called (in that "general practice") to do lots of different things, including the giving of pastoral care, it is also clear that some pastors are more gifted and called than others.

While this little book is directed at the general practitioner, it must be admitted that when one accepts the special gift of pastoral caregiving, it may indeed be at the expense of other avenues within ministry.

Pastors who accept the gift and call of intensive pastoral caregiving are less likely to be "on track" to be the senior pastor of one of the "exemplary mega-churches."

This is not to say that such pastors do not have growing churches. Indeed, I am of the strongest opinion that good pastoral caregiving is what most people seek in a church home. And, when word of excellence in pastoral caregiving gets spread one by one, growth potential is there. However, pastors, whose primary orientation is toward pastoral caregiving, are of a mind to concern themselves much more with "the root structure" of the Church, and allow the fruit bearing to come about naturally. The growth and health of root structure are much like the characteristic Saint Paul wrote about to the Corinthian church – the *fragrance of Christ*. (2 Corinthians 2:15) Unlike the other senses which can be measured (taste – calories and fat grams/yum!; touch – psi; sight – 20/20; sound – decibels) fragrance is not measurable so as to be put into some computer database or chart. But, if the growth of the root structure is nourished, the fruit will grow, by God's work.

Pastors especially gifted in pastoral caregiving are not going to be spending the time and energy that other pastors invest in keeping up with the literature and training events dedicated to "church [*numerical*] growth." One of the interesting "nuggets" uncovered in a presently popular "church growth" program[4] is that the leaders and visionaries of nu-

---

[4]   The *Natural Church Development* program is heavily based on extensive research, from churches all over Christendom. I would note that this "church growth" program is somewhat distinctive from others in that its primary focus in on *organic* growth, rather than *numeric* growth. Christian A. Schwarz, *Natural Church Development, A Guide to Eight Essential Qualities of Healthy Churches* (St. Charles, IL: ChurchSmart Resources, 2000)

merically growing churches tend to not be "people people." They get others to handle that ministry. Their gifts are more oriented towards casting/catching a vision and/or the organizational skills required to execute that vision.

How the pastor in a local church *sees* and *practices* pastoral caregiving also has a direct impact on how they do other parts of their ministry – specifically on their preaching, their understanding and administration of the sacraments, and their prophetic role in the community.

This book will delve into some of those specifics in the following chapters. Additionally, it should be noted that the intensive pastoral caregiver tends toward seeing all phases of her/his ministry in terms of being a healing agent. Never is there a sermon preached or worship led, in which there is not laid out some word of hope. Every worship I lead is inspired by the notion that there may indeed be just one person there that day, whose appearance there is the last chance they're giving to God and the Church to provide some reason why not to commit suicide. If that sounds macabre, it is not meant to be. It's just a metaphoric focal point for the extremely serious business we are about.

Every act as a pastor keeps in the discernment background the notion that I am bound to never allow my personal (theological, political, social, familial, preferential) agenda to become a barrier so as to prevent one of the flock from feeling that they can call upon me as *their pastor* in time of need. That does not mean that the *kerygma* preached and taught is spineless or milquetoast. Rather, it means that it must be done with great humility and respect.

My job as a pastor is not to "tell them what THE truth is." My job as a pastor is not to "fix them." My job as a pastor is to be a guide, who loves his people, and walks alongside them, pointing to signs that God is "in this direction," and inviting them to "walk alongside" that we may walk together with Jesus as our Friend, in search of healing and wholeness together – of self, of the Church, of the community, and of the rift between sinful humans and creation.

Most of all, it means that my primary work *and identity* must be as a *person of prayer*. It is the stock of my trade, it is the guide of my decision making, and it is the food of my soul.

A Nugget

[MORDECAI TO ESTHER:]
*"Who knows? Perhaps you
have come to royal dignity for
just such a time as this."*

(Esther 4:14b)

Remember: we may not be the best qualified to do this, but we are the ones who are here and who have the responsibility of doing it. We can't wait until the best qualified ones come along. Right now, in this place, at this time, we <u>are</u> the best qualified ones to do it.

Bishop S. Clifton Ives

15

3
GOD BLESS THE DONATISTS
(EX OPERE OPERATO)

Unless the LORD builds the house, those who build it labor in vain. Unless the LORD guards the city, the guard keeps watch in vain. It is in vain that you rise up early and go late to rest, eating the bread of anxious toil; for he gives sleep to his beloved. (Psalm 127:1-2)

There come times in pastoral ministry when you will chuckle to yourself about the little one liner you often throw about (to your wife's chagrin, because she is afraid that people will believe it) how "I only work one day a week, and then folks get upset if I work past noon on that day." You chuckle about it to yourself on those days that begin at 6:15 in the morning, and you don't get home from those "blessed" administrative meetings until 9:30 at night, and you still have two emergency pastoral care telephone calls to make before it gets too late (*i.e.* before you and your mate get to eat the carry in pizza you picked up on the way home.)

You chuckle when you think about it running from one place to the next, realizing that while it does seem crazy today, it *really* is a good job – no, not a "good job" but a *great calling*.

If you have too many days in a row like this, it means that (a) you will burn out and won't be able to believe this for very long; (b) you have not done a good job in following the instructions given later in this book; (c) you may have some codependency problems that seriously need attention; or (d) all of the above, plus a few other possibilities.

I remember one day, when I wasn't chuckling as I went through it – at least, not until I remembered those blessed Donatists.

I began the day with a regularly scheduled commitment with a parishioner – following up on a promise that I had made him, to being a covenant partner in following his doctor's advice. We walked together a number of mornings each week – beginning at 6:15 a.m. (Yeah, sure, I was only doing it for him; it wasn't like I didn't need the exercise myself!)

After dropping him off back at his house, and walking home myself, I remembered that today was the day for my regularly scheduled trip to the retirement home for worship and Holy Communion. As I entered the house through the garage, something seemed different. My keen mind, sharply awakened by the brisk walk figured it out after standing in the garage and gawking about for about 30 seconds. Oh, yes; that's it: the garage is empty. I don't have a car. (It was still in the repair shop, the work started yesterday having not been completed.)

Not a problem. I've been talking about riding my bicycle to work; they do it in Europe all the time. About time I got myself in better shape. Hmmm, about that going to the retirement home?? And I need to get communion bread.

Not a problem. Mixed up the bread recipe (without the water – to be added later) put it into a Tupperware container and use the bread maker at the Church. Got dressed, put the Tupperware into the backpack along with the suit coat, and enjoyed the ride through the downtown Charleston traffic. I really did appreciate it; and, besides I gave some of the morning rush hour traffic an opportunity to do a bit of extra praying as they lined up behind me on the bridge, where none could pass me. I even think I heard some of them using the Lord God's Name a couple of times.

In to work. Put the bread mix in. Hit the timer. Go do the crammed activities of the morning, and it will be ready just about time for me to go. I love it when a plan comes together. Five minutes before I leave, I pull the bread out. Uh-oh. This bread maker doesn't quite work like the one at home – this stuff is darker than dark, and it feels hard as a rock. Oh, not to worry; it's probably soft, fluffy and tasty inside.

It is a pretty simple format that I follow at the retirement home – a brief devotional time – which for me usually involves storytelling, and then the ecumenical group shares in the blessed sacrament of Holy Communion. On this day, I had a special treat for them.

I brought a new Communion chalice to our little makeshift altar table. A couple from the church had brought it as a gift to me from their recent trip to the Holy Land. It was made of olive wood and displayed an intricately carved Last Supper, that rolled all around the cup's outer surface – just like in the da Vinci picture: everyone lined up on one side, so nobody's back is in the picture.

After setting out the brown brick that I hoped would actually look like bread on the inside, I decided to draw the focus of their attention away from the brick as I poured the grape juice into the new olive wood piece of art, by telling them the history and love behind the new chalice that I was using for the first time with them.

As I launched into the story I had prepared for the devotion, my eye inadvertently was caught by something strange there on the altar table to my left. The grape juice (not yet consecrated as the blessed Blood of our Lord) was running down the side of the chalice and onto its base. I tried to keep going with the prepared story nonchalantly, but could not help myself from the increasingly frequent and decreasingly furtive glances to the chalice. The little rivulet that seemed to be coming from just below the one apostle's foot (was that Judas?) and running through the squiggly carvings was now forming a small pool on the altar table.

It's hard – I don't know if you've ever tried it – to keep telling a story – keeping the inflection rhythm on track (much of the art of good storytelling) – while at the same time, trying to find the dish towel that you had used to wrap up a brown brick and had put somewhere else, and unobtrusively placing it under the chalice to attempt to stem the flow of purple juice from running from its now deep pool on the altar table onto the carpet below.

Finally the story was over. I didn't feel like I had quite given it my best effort, and we launched into the liturgy of the blessed sacrament. I tried to gauge when the dear folks would be looking down at their liturgy handouts for the longest, as my opportunity to quietly locate the grape juice bottle and replenish the cup. The level was now almost down to the bottom of Judas' foot – well below the comfort level for bread dipping. (We used the intinction method.)

Then came the moment of truth – the breaking of the bread. Did I say "breaking"? I needed a chisel or, perhaps, I was afraid, a chain saw. I'd never wrestled with such a "rock" before. I noticed that some of my beloved seniors were trying to suppress open laughter at my discomfort by this point. I quickly surmised that some of them had noticed the bleeding chalice, as well.

This day was not going well. I was not fit to be the Vicar of Christ, in this very moment. I came just "that close" to allowing negative energy to well up and splash over me like a broken chalice.

And then … I suddenly remembered the Donatists.

I sometimes wondered, back during seminary classes, just what was the point of some of the stuff they were teaching. For example, what possible good would it do my ministry to know that back somewhere around the fourth century there had been a church conference to resolve the great controversy about the Donatist heresy. It was called a "heresy" after the conference. It always works that way, you know. Beforehand, it was an issue between two sides. After they slugged it out in the conference, and took the vote, one side (the winners) emerged as orthodox and the other side (the losers, the Donatists) emerged as the heretics.

Even before taking a church history class, I knew that there had been a time of persecution of the Church by some of the Roman emperors. You remember: *"Renounce Jesus or become dinner for the lions."* For those of us who have never looked into the jaws of a hungry lion, we accepted, as natural, the faith of those faithful ones who kept the lions fat and sassy. Before that class, I had never asked the *Paul-Harvey-rest-of-the-story* question: "What became of those who renounced Jesus, and walked away from the lions' supper table?"

In that church history class, I learned that a good number of these survivors later felt bad about that decision. But not many went running back to the arena, begging to be put onto the menu. Actually, some of them didn't get around to repenting of their renunciation until a new emperor was on the throne. But, repent some of them indeed did. And they repented with gusto – becoming ordained clergy in the Church.

Then along came the Donatists. I suspect that many of them were descendants of the lion dinners of former days. At any rate, they had a burr under their saddle about these former renunciating, but now repentant, Christians serving as pastors. Like Pharisees of Jesus' day, they attacked the "legality" of these pastors' work.

They raised the allegation: "You know; these people renounced Jesus. There's no way they can be the Vicar of Christ. It's not just a disgrace to the Church, but *it taints their administration of the sacraments.* And, oh by the way, Mr. and Mrs. Parent, did you realize that your little baby is going to go to hell because his/her Baptism was not effective. It was done by 'a renouncer'!"

Well, it worked. Those feisty Donatists got enough parents (and others) upset, that a great big stink rose up to the upper echelons of the Church hierarchy.

Does the title of this chapter say, "God bless the Donatists"? Yes, indeed. Those judgmental, no-room-for-grace-nor-forgiveness, self-righteous, uptight Donatists? Yes, that's them. God bless them. Why?

Bless them, because most of our doctrines in the Church arose out of some heresy that needed resolution. How could the Church both reassure the parents who worried about the eternal salvation or damnation of their infant children whom they had, in good conscience, already had baptized, <u>and</u> not get too cozy with those former faint-hearted Christians?

They worked their way through it by the wonderful doctrine of *ex opere operato*. (When dealing with a tricky issue, it's always better to put it in Latin!) Those three words are functionally translated like this:

You know, the power of the work of God in the holy mystery of the sacraments is so strong, that it doesn't really matter what kind of dufus administers it. We do our best to ordain only proper and fit people as clergy to celebrate the sacraments. But, hey, if we mess up, that doesn't mean God's hands are tied. The sacraments work by themselves. Period. You never have to look behind them to see if they are valid. They are valid and efficacious in and of themselves.

(See why they put it into Latin, and why they have left it there? *"Ex opere operato"* works, and it sounds a lot neater, too.)

So, there in the midst of a dripping Judas' foot chalice, while wrestling with a brick that was intended to be a loaf of bread, I remembered out of the clear blue: *ex opere operato!!* God bless those grace-stingy Donatists.

And then I realized: that's why they taught me that stuff in seminary. Those brilliant seminary professors knew that the day would come when – I wouldn't renounce Jesus, but – I would (for whatever reason) feel like such a dolt, that I was not worthy to be the Vicar of Christ. They somehow knew that the day would come when I would feel like such a stumblebum that I would believe I was ruining the work of God.

Ex opere operato!! God uses me. And God will make up for my mistakes. In fact, sometimes, God even chooses to work *through* my mistakes. That day -- God *was* present at our Holy Communion feast, and God really did bless us with a *very* holy mystery.

Serving as a pastoral caregiver involves *ex opere operato*, too. We don't have to always have "it" figured out. We don't always have to have the right answers. We don't always have to say the right things. God works through our weaknesses. In fact, I have found (*ex opere operato!*) that sometimes when I feel the most inadequate, and most ill-prepared to deal with a pastoral care need, this is when God works most effectively through me.

We *always* need to do our best to be good pastoral caregivers. But we *also* need to understand that God is not limited by our limitations. Be there. Listen to God's directions. And don't worry, if you have not figured it all out. Remember: *ex opere operato!*

A Nugget

USE JESUS' BLESSED MIRROR

One of the greatest tools that Jesus used was His blessed mirror. It isn't specifically mentioned in the Gospels, but even a casual reading of the Gospels reveals how over and over, He would reach into the inside pocket of his robe and pull out this Blessed Mirror, that was unlike any other of its time.

This mirror showed people both the Image of God in which they were indeed lovingly made. And it showed them their potential.

The first image that appears is that of a "beloved child of God, precious and beautiful to behold." Then they will be able to see a Crown of Glory over their heads – an image that they can spend the rest of their lives growing up until they fit into that Crown. They can do so, by God's Grace and because someone showed them what it looks like.

Because Jesus has shown you this image of yourself, you, too, therefore, are able to show others the same thing. Helping them to see this is the greatest gift you can give them.

4

The idols of the nations are silver and gold, the work of human hands. They have mouths, but they do not speak; they have eyes, but they do not see; they have ears, but they do not hear, and there is no breath in their mouths. Those who make them and all who trust them shall become like them.
(Psalm 135:15-18)

One of the most powerful forces working in our people's lives today is a sense of disconnectedness. They are disconnected from one another; they are disconnected from God. They spend much time and energy looking for that which will make them whole, make them feel complete. I'm not convinced that this is only a contemporary phenomenon; I don't know for sure. But it surely is real.

Sometimes the Church seeks to answer that basic hunger, by making folks search for a sense of being "righteous," as an answer to their need for being whole, of being connected to God. Much of the time, that search for "righteousness" begins with an acknowledgement of sinfulness: "We can't receive God's Grace so necessary for our salvation,

27

until we first recognize our sinfulness, our brokenness, our separation from God."

And so it is. But, it seems to me that, at least today, most people don't already realize their brokenness. Even people who appear to be smug and self-centered, and altogether (but together only in themselves) – even these people, I believe, are only using that arrogance, that persona, to mask the brokenness that they feel inside.

Most people do not come to Church, or need a pastor, to tell them that they are bad, that they don't have it together as they should. I am reminded of a colleague who shared with me his experience with a woman who made her living selling her body. She was sick, broke, and feeling helpless and hopeless. He invited her to come to Church. And her response struck him powerfully: "Church?" she said. "With all of the problems I've got in my life, why would I want to add to them by coming to Church, to be told what a loser I am."

If, as pastors (and hence leaders of the Church) we cast an image of the Body of Christ as being one of Judgment, then we cannot provide the balm in Gilead that so many need.

Our role as pastoral caregivers – AND as leaders of the Church – depends on which model we follow with our ministry, AND in our personal living. We can choose between two:

- IF – THEN
  OR
- BECAUSE -- THEREFORE

THE "IF – THEN" MODEL

The first model is one that the world so often uses. If you do this, then I will do the following. It is the *quid pro quo* way of doing business. It gets lived out in so much of our lives that we don't even recognize it. (At the end of your reading of the discussion of this model for life, I invite you to set the book down, and think back upon your own life over the past week, or even just the past 24 hours. Remember your activities; think upon each of your personal encounters with others, and meditate upon how much of all of this is driven by the *If – then* way of handling life.)

The *If – then* approach to life is, among other things, a way of *attempting* to maintain control over life, to keep balance, to not be taken advantage of.

It is also the way of Satan.

A brief understanding of Satan is necessary. We so often think of Satan as "The Tempter." We see a different perspective in the prologue to the book of Job.

> [6]One day the heavenly beings came to present themselves before the LORD, and Satan[£] also came among them. [7]The LORD said to Satan, "Where have you come from?" Satan answered the LORD, "From going to and fro on the earth, and from walking up and down on it." [8]The LORD said to Satan, "Have you considered my servant Job? There is no one like him on the earth, a blameless and upright man who fears God and turns away from evil."

Satan is portrayed here as one who (in my way of understanding) is something akin to a Prosecuting Attorney of Creation: He goes too and fro, looking for inadequacies, challenging, making accusations. For example, when God holds up the poster child of righteousness, Job, Satan challenges:

> [9]Then Satan answered the LORD, "Does Job fear God for nothing? [10]Have you not put a fence around him and his house and all that he has, on every side? You have blessed the work of his hands, and his possessions have increased in the land. [11]But stretch out your hand now, and touch all that he has, and he will curse you to your face."

In other words, Satan says that Job is good only because he gets goodies. And then he follows up with his favorite tool – the *If – then* scenario: **If** you take away Job's goodies (blessings) **then** Job will not be such a poster child for you ("will curse you to your face.")

It is a role that we see Satan also playing when Jesus entered into the wilderness for forty days, immediately following His Baptism.

> **If** you are the Son of God, **then** turn these stones into bread. … **If** you are the Son of God, **then** jump off this steeple and let the angels hold you up.

The Voice of Satan is always the Voice of Accusation, always speaking in terms of *If – then*. We are told in Luke's

Gospel that after Satan "*had finished every test, he depart-ed from [Jesus] <u>until an opportune time</u>.*" (Luke 4:13)

Now, as every good pastoral caregiver knows, timing is very important. (And, as discussed shortly, the timing of Satan's testing of Jesus in the wilderness, set immediately after Jesus' Baptism, is critical to our understanding.)

When was that opportune time? We don't have another reference made to Satan testing Jesus again in the Gospels. We don't need to have Satan specifically identified by name, however, when we know how Satan works.

> [35]And the people stood by, watching; but the leaders scoffed at him, saying, "He saved others; let him save himself if he is the Messiah of God, his chosen one!" [36]The soldiers also mocked him, coming up and offering him sour wine, [37]and saying, "If you are the King of the Jews, save yourself!" [38]There was also an inscription over him, "This is the King of the Jews."

> [39]One of the criminals who were hanged there kept deriding him and saying, "Are you not the Messiah? Save yourself and us!" (Luke 23)

Satan throws his voice so that it comes through the mouths of the leaders, of the soldiers, and of the one thief on the cross. Each time the satanic message is the same, and the same as it was in the testing in the wilderness: *If you are the Messiah / King of the Jews, <u>then</u> save yourself / save us*.

The voice of Satan is always the voice of Accusation – "prove yourself!"

John Wesley's own journal gives testimony to this very thing. On the morning of May 25, 1738, after the experience the night before, when his heart was strangely warmed at the meeting on Aldersgate Street, Wesley wrote:

> The moment I awaked, 'Jesus, Master,' was in my heart and in my mouth; and I found all my strength lay in keeping my eye fixed upon him, and my soul waiting on him continually. ... *Yet the enemy injected a fear, 'If you do believe, [then] why is there not a more sensible change?'*[5]

---

[5]   Ward and Heitzenrater, ed. *The Words of John Wesley (Bicentennial edition) vol. 18, Journals and Diaries I (1735-1738)* (Nashville: Abingdon Press, 1988) p. 251.

Satan's tendency is always to use the *If – Then* approach. It undermines our confidence in God's working in our lives. It always emphasizes that God's work has to fit into our own expectations. It denies the notion that God works through a growing process; Satan always wants us to believe that there must be an instantaneous result.

The *If – Then* approach to life is also the way that most people think that they are able to find satisfaction in life, to find the connectedness they seek, to find Peace. It works like this:

- If only I could get this job, then I would have enough money to provide for my needs.
- If only I can achieve this goal, then the rest of my life will work well.
- If only the test result comes back negative, then I will surely thank God and make sure that I turn my life around and get to Church every Sunday.
- If only I could get the right appointment, then I know that I could do good ministry.
- If only whatever it is, then surely I can have whatever I need.

The *If – Then* approach to life <u>always</u> makes our Peace circumstantial. It always depends on the circumstances in which we live: Good circumstances and we feel good; bad circumstances and we feel lousy.

And this is one of the great challenges we face as pastoral caregivers. People are always looking for the fulfillment of the *If* in their lives, so that *then* they can be at peace. They often come to us when the circumstances have hit rock bottom, when it doesn't seem like there is any possible good *then* that can come into their lives.

Sometimes, it takes just that very set of circumstances before people are able or willing to receive the *Good News* that Jesus came to give:

Peace I leave with you; My Peace I give to you. I do not give to you as the world gives. (John 14:27)

The peace that the world gives is always *If – Then* peace. It always depends on the circumstances. It is always living from the outside inward. Jesus' Peace is different. It is lived from the inside outward. It is based upon *Because – Therefore*.

THE "BECAUSE -- THEREFORE" MODEL

Jesus was tested by Satan, with the *If – Then* paradigm for life, immediately after His Baptism. In His, Baptism, Jesus heard a different way of communicating. After He came up from out of the water, the Voice from Heaven said:

"This is my Son, the Beloved, with whom I am well pleased." (Matthew 3:17)

When Jesus was baptized, He established how CHRISTIAN BAPTISM is no longer the same. No longer was it just about repentance - as had been the Baptism that John the Baptist was offering in the Jordan River. Jesus had nothing for which to repent. No, He was the new prototype - showing us that Baptism is about Identity. What was spoken at Jesus' Baptism is what God says at EACH OF OUR BAPTISMS - you ARE my beloved child with whom I am well pleased. Can we grasp what a difference that makes?

Janet Wolf, one of our very gifted United Methodist storytellers explains it like this:

> In a world that pronounces so many of us "not good enough," what might it mean to believe that we really are chosen, precious, and beloved? In a new members' class, we talked about baptism: this holy moment when we are named by God's grace with such power it won't come undone.
>
> Fayette was there - a woman living on the streets, struggling with mental illness and lupus. She loved the part about baptism and would ask over and over, "And when I'm baptized, I am ...?" We soon learned to respond, "Beloved child of God, precious and beautiful to behold." "Oh, yes!" she'd say, and then we could go back to our discussion.
>
> The big day came. Fayette went under, came up spluttering, and cried, "And now I am ...?" And we all sang, "Beloved child of God, precious and beautiful

to behold." "Oh, yes!" she shouted as she danced all around the fellowship hall.

Two months later I got a call. Fayette had been beaten and raped and was at the county hospital. So I went. I could see her from a distance, pacing back and forth. When I got to the door, I heard, "I am beloved ..." She turned, saw me, and said, "I am beloved child of God, precious and ..." Catching sight of herself in the mirror - hair sticking up, blood and tears streaking her face, dress torn, dirty and rebuttoned askew, she started again, "I am beloved child of God, precious and ..." She looked in the mirror again and declared "... and God is still working on me. If you come back tomorrow, I'll be so beautiful I'll take your breath away!"[6]

Our Baptism - the Jesus kind - is when we, too, receive that blessing - when the Voice from Heaven names us and claims us: This is My Beloved Child in Whom I am well Pleased.

One of our primary tasks as pastoral caregivers is to get people to understand (in their hearts, not just in their heads) that just like Fayette: God made us in God's very Own Image. And God is well pleased with God's Own handiwork.

When we come to understand - in our hearts - not just in our heads - that we are MADE IN GOD'S OWN IMAGE the difference can be transforming.

Because I am a beloved child of God, precious and beautiful to behold *therefore* I am able to face whatever confronts me.

The theological doctrine *Imago Dei* (made in God's image) finds its biblical roots in the Creation story – at Genesis 1:27. Just what that means is the subject of much theological discussion. Pastoral caregiving absolutely requires us to "do theology." But effective pastoral caregiving rarely involves talking like the scholarly theologians do.

So I have come to think of the *Imago Dei* – being made in God's image – claiming the promise of Fayette: "beloved child of God, precious and beautiful to behold" as simply as this:

---

[6]   *Companions in Christ (Leader's Guide)* (Nashville: Upper Room Books, 2001) pp. 36-37. See also *Questions of Faith, vol. V* (Nashville: EcuFilms, 1994)

WE ARE A CHIP OFF THE OLD BLOCK.

For this image, I think of a stone mason chipping away on a piece of marble. As he chips away at the stone, none of the pieces coming off the original block are uniform; each is different. And each piece of that block fits perfectly, and only, into the place from which it was chipped. But each piece of marble chip is every bit a piece of marble, just like the original whole block of marble.

St. Augustine is often quoted:

We are restless, O God, until we find our rest in Thee."

So it is for each one of us, made in the very Image of God. We are not at home; we are not connected; we do not have Peace – until we are fitted back into the block from which we have been chipped.

Because I am a *chip off the old block*, *therefore* I have a place in God, where I fit, where I belong, where I am at home.

Because I am a *chip off the old block – a beloved child of God, precious and beautiful in God's eyes to behold*, *therefore* I don't have to earn God's blessing; I already have it.

The theological lesson is important – but if it remains just in the head, then it doesn't do very much good. It has to move *THE LONGEST FOURTEEN INCHES IN THE WORLD* – from the head to the heart. But, when it is heart knowledge, it can make all the difference.

Fred Craddock, while lecturing at Yale University, told of going back home one summer to Gatlinburg, Tennessee, to take a short vacation with his wife. One night they found a quiet little restaurant where they looked forward to a private meal-just the two of them.

While they were waiting for their meal they noticed a distinguished looking, white-haired man moving from table to table, visiting guests. Craddock whispered to his wife, "I hope he doesn't come over here." He didn't want the man to intrude on their privacy. But the man did come by his table.

"Where you folks from?" he asked amicably.

"Oklahoma."

"Splendid state, I hear, although I've never been there. What do you do for a living?

"I teach homiletics at the graduate seminary of Phillips University."

"Oh, so you teach preachers, do you. Well, I've got a story I want to tell you." And with that he pulled up a chair and sat down at the table with Craddock and his wife.

Dr. Craddock said he groaned inwardly: Oh no, here comes another preacher story. It seems everyone has one.

The man stuck out his hand. "I'm Ben Hooper. I was born not far from here across the mountains. My mother wasn't married when I was born so I had a hard time. When I started to school my classmates had a name for me, and it wasn't a very nice name. I used to go off by myself at recess and during lunch-time because the taunts of my playmates cut so deeply.

"What was worse was going downtown on Saturday afternoon and feeling every eye burning a hole through you. They were all wondering just who my real father was.

"When I was about 12 years old a new preacher came to our church. I would always go in late and slip out early. But one day the preacher said the benediction so fast I got caught and had to walk out with the crowd. I could feel every eye in church on me. Just about the time I got to the door I felt a big hand on my shoulder. I looked up and the preacher was looking right at me.

"Who are you, son? Whose boy are you?'

I felt the old weight come on me. It was like a big black cloud. Even the preacher was putting me down.

But as he looked down at me, studying my face, he began to smile a big smile of recognition. "Wait a minute," he said, "I know who you are. I see the family resemblance. You are a son of God."

With that he slapped me across the rump and said, "Boy you've got a great inheritance. Go and claim it."

The old man looked across the table at Fred Craddock and said, "That was the most important single sentence ever said to me." With that he smiled, shook the hands of Craddock and his wife, and moved on to another table to greet old friends.

Suddenly, Fred Craddock remembered. On two occasions the people of Tennessee had elected an illegitimate to be their governor. One of them was Ben Hooper.[7]

Our growth as Christians is <u>NOT</u> as so many seem to think - being that which we can accomplish if we try hard enough. Rather it is about becoming more of what we already are.

If I plant an oak sapling in my yard, I do not come inside and tell my wife that I just planted 1/20th of an oak tree. Although that little tree, given good nurture and care, will grow to more than 20 times the size of that little sapling, nonetheless, what I planted was an oak tree, not 1/20th of an oak tree.

Because I am a beloved child of God, precious and beautiful to behold, *therefore* I can become all that I need in life to become. I can have peace, irrespective of what my life circumstances are, because of this.

My *because* is my identity, my inside. When I claim that identity, then it shapes my circumstances, my outside. I can live from the inside out, instead of how my world teaches me to live from the outside in. I can indeed know that peace that passes all understanding, that which Jesus gives, which is not as the world gives.

When as a pastoral caregiver, we are called to help

- those in need,
- those who hunger for connectedness,
- those whose life circumstances make them think that peace is impossible,
- those for whom the circumstances in life threaten to completely overwhelm them, we can give them more help than by any other means, when we walk with them on that longest fourteen inches of the world, as they learn to trust the very truth in their heart, that they are a "chip off the old block."

---

[7]   Craddock; (Graves and Ward, ed.) *Craddock Stories* (St. Louis: Chalice Press, 2001)

We don't have to overcome all of the "*if* only's" of accomplishment; instead we only have to grow into what we already are.

[Because of] the power at work within us [therefore we can] accomplish abundantly far more than all we can ask or imagine! (Ephesians 3:20)

A Nugget

YOU DON'T HAVE TO HAVE THE

RIGHT ANSWER INSTANTLY.

One of the most important ingredients in a pastoral caregiving setting is the honesty and genuineness of you, the pastoral caregiver.

It helps to establish trust.

It models for the recipient how Grace works lovingly.

If you are confronted with a question (where is this in scripture, what do you think God means by this, and a whole host of other hard questions) that either (a) you don't know the answer and/or (b) you are not comfortable with the answer that pops into your head or heart as being what God wants to be the answer for this setting then do not be reluctant to admit that you want some more time to "chew on this" in your own heart and study <u>and</u> in your conversation <u>with the Boss</u>. (Remember, your purpose is to love your people, love your people, love your people – <u>not</u> to impress them with how erudite you are.)

But don't use this as a dodge of a tough issue. Do just what you said: chew on this in your own heart and study <u>and </u>in your conversation <u>with the Boss</u>. And make sure that you get back with the person to talk about it some more … to help them find their own answer, that works for <u>them</u> and <u>the Boss</u>.

5
"IT'S NOT ABOUT ME"

Abba Romanos was at the point of death, and his disciples were gathered around his death bed. They asked him, "How ought we conduct ourselves?"

The old man said to them, "I do not think I have ever told one of you to do something without having first made the decision not to get angry, if what I said were not done; and so we have lived in peace all our days."

How well we do what we are supposed to do has a lot to do with how well those in our flock will be enabled to find peace in their lives – a full *Shalom* (wholeness, completeness, spiritual-physical-mental-emotional congruency) peace.

But how well we do has a lot to do with us remembering: "It's not about me" and I need to get me out of the way in order to let God do Her thing.

Let me tell you a story about Freddy. Like all good stories must, it begins with: "Once upon a time, …

41

… there was a man named Freddy. Freddy was a good man and had grown up in a good, Christian home. He had – as some would describe it, a "drug problem" in his early years. Whenever his mother or father went to worship, they "drug Freddy" along. He was with his parents in church whenever the church door was open – worship, Sunday School, revivals, special worship, youth meetings – Freddy always managed to be "drug there."

But he didn't resent it. It was a way of life which he not only considered "normal," but also was something in which he found both enjoyment and great meaning.

Freddy met a girl (whose name doesn't really have to be mentioned) in the Church. They dated all through high school and college, and were married shortly afterwards. But – as these things sometimes turn out – even though Freddy thought he knew her very well, a short while into the marriage, Freddy discovered that his wife wasn't just who he thought she was. She had a serious drinking problem, which only grew worse, not better – regardless of how much Freddy tried to help her out, tried to get her help, and prayed about it. After a few years of marriage, Freddy's wife left him for another man, and also left him with a mountain of debt.

I didn't know Freddy then – actually, it was before my time. I only heard about this part of Freddy's life from other folks. They said that Freddy was devastated by all that happened in his failed marriage. But they also said that Freddy would often be heard to say: *"I am in the Potter's Hands; what God has in store for me is better than I can ask or imagine."*

Freddy never remarried, and he never had children. He seemed to be content to invest, what he would have given to his children, into the children of the Church. He worked hard with the youth group, and became a real role model for them. He gave his time tirelessly – even after the age when many adults seem to get the notion that it's time for someone else to get involved, and they quit working with the children and the youth.

Then one time – and this was after I got to know Freddy, when he worked with my youth group – one of the teenagers told a story about Freddy – said that he had done something they called "inappropriate" with her. (Her name isn't really important.) Word moved like wildfire around the church – as rumors of something bad seem to always move faster in the church than stories about anything good. I couldn't believe it. Not Freddy!

He never said anything in his own defense. I went and talked to him about it. All he would tell me was: *"Things aren't always what they seem. We'll leave it in the Potter's hands. What God has in store is better than we can ever ask or imagine."*

I was furious, when I finally talked to the girl and found out that she had made the whole story up. I'm not a psychologist, but I think she just wanted some attention. By the time the whole thing got worked out, her parents (not her, although I thought it should have been!) made a public apology in the Church, and Freddy was cleared – although I know that there are some people who, once they get a bad idea about someone in their heads, they have a hard time letting go of it.

But – for the most part – Freddy's honor and reputation were restored. And the Church learned some very important lessons, in the process.

And Freddy – well, he just kept on doing what he had always done. He just loved to do things for other people.

Freddy got cancer a few years after that. Actually, the diagnosis was made during a routine exam, but the doctor recommended that they not do anything about it – just watch it, for six months, and see what happened. It's hard for me to believe it – even today – with all that we hear about the importance of early detection. But six months later, Freddy's cancer had spread so much that what could have been treated, with a fairly good prognosis, was now in a very advanced stage. I know that there were lawyers in the Church who recommended that Freddy file a malpractice action.

But Freddy wouldn't hear of it. He just said, "What's done is done. What I've got to do – all any of us can do – is just deal with the present moment. No sense re-hashing old history. And, besides -- things aren't always what they seem. We'll leave it in the Potter's hands. What God has in store is better than we can ever ask or imagine."

I was well beyond being a youth at this point, but I think I was closer to Freddy then than before. It just amazed me to see his faith in action. As his body was wasting away, he still kept on coming to Church. It got to the point where that was all that he was able to do – just come to worship. He was no longer able to do any other work in the Church. But his faithfulness was such a powerful testimony to his faith. He had no idea of how much his life had meant to so many people. And he really had no idea of what an impact it had on people that he just showed up.

It got to the point, however, when Freddy was no longer able to even come to worship. I visited with him regularly. I'll never forget our conversation that one day:

"You know, I'm having a hard time dealing with this now. I've spent my whole life loving Jesus, and I've always enjoyed being able to help others. But, now, I'm not able to help anyone. Now, I have to rely upon people coming in to help me. At first I had a hard time accepting that help. I really did! And then I remembered: *things aren't always what they seem. We'll leave it in the Potter's hands. What God has in store is better than we can ever ask or imagine.* And I finally realized that this, too, is an important lesson for me to learn. If I don't know how to receive, even when I can't give, then I'm not ready to receive my very own salvation – because that's totally a gift. And so – even though my pride didn't like the idea to begin with, now I know. This, too, is a precious gift from God.

Freddy died not long after we had that conversation. I guess he had taken the final course, in that lifetime academy of preparing a soul for eternity.

Not all of the lessons that came in his school of hard knocks were just for his own personal growth. Some of them were for the people around him. And even this great man himself still needed to be re-molded and re-shaped himself, to receive the final blessing in his last few days – to fit him for eternity.

- IT TAKES A WHOLE LIFETIME TO PREPARE A SOUL FOR ETERNITY

- IT'S NOT ABOUT <u>ME</u>. Sometimes the Potter uses the stuff of our lives to help others be re-molded and re-shaped.

What a blessing I have received from all the Freddies in my life – who have truly been the wind beneath my wings. His life helps me remember that "it's not about me."

Not every pastor finds it within their heart to be like Freddie. I have been called upon throughout my ministry to go into several churches as a "conflict management" specialist of some sort, to help them work through various and different conflicts. I have also been a careful listener to "preacher stories" during my whole lifetime (both before and after I entered pastoral ministry.) One common thread that often is found in cases of church conflict and of pastors who continually have difficult appointments is the issue of "respect for the office of pastor." The pastor seems to feel that s/he is not receiving the respect that s/he deserves. That can be a problem. Too often it points to a pastor who has not mastered the lesson: *It's not about me*.

A colleague in ministry once told about the day when he went to the hospital to call on a sick parishioner. As, too often is the case, he was in a bit of a hurry, he grew frustrated when he could not find a parking place in the hospital parking lot. After driving around a few times, he finally spied one, some distance away. As he bore down on the parking spot, he noticed, in his peripheral vision, another car aimed for the same place. He pushed down on the accelerator, cut off the other car, nearly caused an accident, and whipped into the parking place.

He noticed that the driver of the other car had a big scowl on his face. But – as the *Blues Brothers said in their movie – He was on a mission for God –* so he didn't worry. He waited until the other car was sufficiently past him, to avoid the need for any confrontation, and then trotted into the hospital. He said the visit went well, and he was about to say a prayer and take his leave, when into the room walked a visitor for the other patient in the room. His eyes and the new visitor's eyes met for just a second, and the pastor's eyes turned away – but not before he noticed that the other man's eyes dropped down to look at his "VISIT-

ING CLERGY" identification badge. Yep, you guessed it: it was the man who drove the car that he had cut off in the parking lot.

He said, that in that embarrassing and humbling moment, he came to understand Jesus' teaching about dinner guests who were humbled after exalting themselves. (Luke 14:7-14) He had – to his own way of thinking – quite legitimately humbled himself, in the parking lot. And, now, he was so humbled/humiliated that he was afraid to leave the room, although he had already announced his intention to do so. He was afraid that this new visitor might just tell his parishioner and visitors what sort of pastor they had.

When you are providing pastoral care, you have got to remember: *It's not about ME*. It's more than about preventing conflict; it's more than about being embarrassed. It's about being a <u>servant</u> minister, which <u>is</u> the calling of each of us.

And <u>it is fundamental to providing good pastoral care</u>.

When you are in pastoral conversation with someone, it is indeed important to listen carefully to their words, to try to get a sense of their feelings. The practice of ACTIVE EMPATHY is critical. The first "working hypothesis" of how a person must be feeling is almost always trying to put yourself into their shoes.

That does <u>not</u> mean, however, that you need to let the person know that you think you know how they feel, by sharing your own similar experience.

A fellow who attended seminary with me has often popped into my mind as a RED FLAG REMINDER during my own pastoral conversations. "Keith" (not his real name) was a careful listener to the details of every conversation. But then he *always* would share how he had a similar life experience. One could never have a conversation with Keith without the notion that he could (and would) "one up" your life experience.

The constancy of Keith's behavior in this regard made him – over time – not a conversation partner of choice. Actually, it took me a while before I figured out what it was about his conversation habits that made me uncomfortable.

I didn't recognize for awhile that it was this constant "one upping" that was the problem.

One day, however, it came into clear focus. It was right after our Wednesday Chapel worship, and a group of us (all women, plus Keith and me) were having conversation in the narthex of the chapel. The conversation between the women turned to a discussion of the monthly visitation of their "female friend."

(I suppose that it was because of the intimacy that develops among seminary students that the conversation did indeed go on in Keith's and my presence. Rather than be embarrassed to be a listening participant in this quite female discussion, I felt good that they were comfortable enough with me to talk about it in my presence.)

Then – out of the clear blue; I mean really from out in left field – Keith (hitherto, like myself, a quiet listening participant in the conversation) suddenly weighed into it. And, honest to goodness, he "one upped" (or tried) their menstruation story with one of his own.

KA-POW! All of the air got sucked out of the immediate atmosphere. No one – absolutely no one – had the faintest idea of how to respond. And in that moment, I suddenly gained the insight of what it was about Keith's conversation habits that I found troubling. But more importantly, I have had this conversational atomic bomb-like experience that registers in my head whenever I start to think about responding to a parishioner with a ... "Oh yes, I know what you mean. Let me tell you about the time when I ...."

Listen carefully. Check in with your parishioner to make sure that (a) you really are hearing correctly what s/he is saying, and (b) to let them know that you are genuinely interested in what they are telling you.

But, remember, It's not about ME. It's about them.

The one exception to this prohibition of sharing your own story is in the introductory "chit chat" phase of a conversation. This is the time when you are getting comfortable with each other; feeling each other out; becoming somewhat vulnerable with some self-disclosure. Here, indeed, it is important to open up. But always, always, always, keep in mind the purpose for doing such. And limit that kind of disclosure to that initial part of the conversation.

One of the real temptations in pastoral counseling is to try to "fix" the person, or to try to "fix" their problem. They may even think that this is why they came to see you. (Please read and re-read "nugget" on *"The Issue is Almost Never THE Issue."*) *(pg. 95)* At least two things are wrong with that approach to pastoral caregiving:

➢ **Your solution may work for you. That is no guarantee (nor even a good predictor) that it will work for this person.** *It's not about ME.*

If we look to just two of the post-resurrection experiences of Jesus in the lives of His disciples, we can see how Jesus prefers individually tailored solutions. To Mary, Jesus told her <u>not</u> to touch Him. She needed to be able to let go of her previous (limited) experience of Jesus, and to grow into experiencing Him in a new way, that went beyond mere physical touch. To Thomas, however, Jesus invited him to "let his fingers do their walking" all over His body – in order to meet his need – to believe that the resurrection was actual and that He was real.

Two apparently opposite positions were taken by Jesus. Each was suited to the person's needs. Too often, we will miss the boat with what is suited to a parishioner's needs when we focus on what worked in our own spiritual life. Our job is to focus on what Jesus wants to do in *their* life, and to help them discover that.

➢ **That which people hear, accept, and remember, is usually what they hear coming from their own lips.** If the discovery of both the REAL issue and the way that they are going to deal with it does not come from within – through their own processing of their life story with God – then it will always be for them *just* Rev'd So-and-so's answer. It won't be theirs. And remember: *It's not about ME.*

"He must increase, but I must decrease." (John 3:30)

Although compassion is good (*a la* the first nugget of this book: three most important rules of doing ministry) remember that EMPATHY is more important to providing good pastoral care than SYMPATHY. It also takes more thinking and feeling and effort. There is indeed the work of feeling, but it is not just "how would I feel.."

First, the pastor must get to where the parishioner has been, in order to grasp where they are now – in order to feel what they feel now. It is, indeed, an inexact art because no one knows what has gone on behind the closed doors of the years of the parishioner's life.

So one must work hard at listening and asking probing, yet not prying, open-ended questions to seek out their present life situation.

The work of the Holy Spirit is critical. A good pastor will have such a close relationship with God through his/her own prayer life that s/he will learn to trust the nudgings of the Spirit. Trust enough to follow the lead in asking questions, but wise enough to not jump to conclusions.

More important to good pastoral caregiving than "figuring the parishioner out" is to help the parishioner to figure themself out in the revealing light of the Holy Spirit.

It's not about me – the pastor. It IS about the parishioner. Our coming to know their exact problem and the perfect solution for it is both impossible and not our goal. Our ability to do such is impeded by the limitations of language, the unwillingness *and* the inability of the parishioner to share all that lies dormant behind the closed doors of their life.

Our goal is not to become "Karnak the Magnificent" That makes it "all about me." Our goal is to be open enough to God's Spirit that we can be the human mechanism through which God can touch their life tenderly and truthfully enough that they will trust enough to open the door of their heart to that same Spirit.

Always, we are only a vessel of God's Spirit and Grace. We are not the parishioner's date. We are just the matchmaker. We invite them to the dance, but are not the dance partner. That is God.

I heard a doctor once say that when he does his job right – taking the time and asking the right questions – the patient (who knows her body better than anyone else) will tell the doctor what her illness is (although the patient's lack of medical training may prevent her from being able to connect all the dots and hence not be able to realize nor recognize the medical answer herself.) The good doctor will, of course, run the normal tests to confirm the diagnosis. But it begins with listening to the patient – taking the time and asking the right questions.

The pastoral caregiver is a doctor – a doctor of the soul. Well, perhaps a better, truer definition is "physician's assistant" to the True Healer – God Who made us. Our job is to just get the Healer and the patient connected.

God is the Healer. Jesus is the Medicine. I am only the Doctor of the Soul. ***It's not about ME***.

A Nugget

THE THREE MOST IMPORTANT

RULES FOR PASTORAL CAREGIVING

<u>AND</u>

FOR EFFECTIVE MINISTRY:

LOVE YOUR PEOPLE.

LOVE YOUR PEOPLE.

LOVE YOUR PEOPLE.

(THESE ARE FOUND IN SCRIPTURE AT JOHN 21:15-17)

- ➤ DON'T EVER FORGET THEM

- ➤ DON'T BE AFRAID TO LET YOUR PEOPLE KNOW THAT THESE ARE YOUR GUIDING PRINCIPLES

- ➤ DON'T TRY TO FAKE THEM; FOLLOW THESE THREE RULES PRAYERFULLY AND GENUINELY ... ALWAYS!

6
AT THE HOSPITAL

^{13c}Be at peace among yourselves. ¹⁴And we urge you, beloved, to admonish the idlers, encourage the fainthearted, help the weak, be patient with all of them. ¹⁵See that none of you repays evil for evil, but always seek to do good to one another and to all. ¹⁶Rejoice always, ¹⁷pray without ceasing, ¹⁸give thanks in all circumstances; for this is the will of God in Christ Jesus for you. ¹⁹Do not quench the Spirit. ²⁰Do not despise the words of prophets, ²¹but test everything; hold fast to what is good; ²²abstain from every form of evil. (1 Thessalonians 5: 13c-22)

What is the "right" thing to do when makin\g a hospital visit?

The first thing is that you should <u>pray *before going into the room*</u>.

- PRAY: as you leave the car,

- PRAY: as you put your pastoral caregiver ID on (yes, it is important to wear that in the hospital – it makes you a legitimate person to be coming into the room, it makes pathways open in [most] hospitals (most of which suffer from various forms of paranoia arising from a monster run amok in the land known as HIPAA) – including getting the room number from the receptionist, and it also serves as an invitation to the poor, distraught person in the hallway to come up to you and ask you to pray for someone you don't know)

- PRAY: as you go to the desk to find out the room number (which you have prepared for before going to the hospital by checking the official membership role to get the formal name of your parishioner, "Bill Smith," (whose real name is Horatio William Smith) because they won't tell you the room number for "Bill Smith" because they don't have anyone by that name; they only have "Horatio Smith."

- PRAY: as you encounter the occasional "unhappy" or "unfriendly" hospital employee. You will be praying for that person because the chances are better than significant that this person is not normally the "bear with a sore head" that they appear to be on this occasion. Your being in prayer, and praying for this person, does not go unnoticed – either consciously or subconsciously or both. Your prayer for that person may indeed be that which they need to help them survive the teenager who lives in their home who replaced the sweet pre-teenager who used to live with them and which has today driven them to the brink of despair before they came into work.

- PRAY: as you get on the elevator, keep praying for the person whom you are coming to visit, as well as for the family members who are with them. And be praying for yourself, as well. Pray for yourself that you will be a vessel for God's grace to flow through you. Pray that you will be observant to the subtle clues of what is going on. Pray that you will not have your own ego so involved that you become a barrier to what God is wanting to do through you.

Now that you are "prayed up," you go into the room. The situation in this moment is quite varied. Sometimes you are visiting someone you know very well. Sometimes it is a shut-in that you may not have ever seen (such as during the early stages of your ministry in a church.) Sometimes it is someone that you are sure you know, but you go into the room, see two beds, and realize that you don't recognize either patient.

Here's a clue: people look different when they are horizontal than vertical. People look different when they are feeling near their very worst, as opposed to how they look on Sunday mornings. People look different in those fashion conscious "things" called "gowns," than in what we have grown accustomed to calling "clothing."

Prior to getting to this point, when you asked at the reception desk for the room number, it's a good idea to ask for the bed number as well – even if you don't think that you will have a problem of recognition (for the reasons begun to be listed in the preceding paragraph) – AND you will ask someone at the hospital how they number their beds. For some hospitals, bed number 1 is by the door and bed number 2 is by the window. In others, it's the opposite. And in one hospital where I visit, bed number 1 is always on the left and bed number 2 is always on the right; it just depends, therefore, on whether the door to the room is to the left or right of the beds.

I remember one time, earlier in my ministry, when I did yet know these principles. I entered the room – no problem: it was a private room. So I didn't bother to check the patient name either on the door, or on the chart holder outside the door, or on the name plate over the bed. I didn't recognize the woman, but I wasn't sure that I would. So, I just launched into the pastoral caregiving. Since I was merely inexperienced, but not completely stupid, it did not take me more than five or ten minutes to pick up enough clues to alert the Sherlock Holmes deep within the recesses of my mind: this was not the woman I had intended on visiting. (After leaving the room, I later found out that "my" patient had been moved to another room, and the change had not yet been entered into the computer.)

After my like-a-steel-trap-mind had reached this deduction, I had to figure out what to do. I was slightly embarrassed at my faux pas, but was not so rattled that I forgot the number one lesson of hospital pastoral caregiving: pray.

And so I did. And the answer I was given was something along the lines of: *Well, you're here. You're a pastoral caregiver. You're my representative. Perhaps, your stupidity is not for naught. Do what needs to be done.*

And, so, that is what I did. Finally, after a delightful time together, I prepared to take my leave. Here, I followed two other important rules of pastoral caregiving (whether in the hospital or not): (1) <u>always</u> speak the truth (at least insofar as you are able to see it) and (2) pray with the person (after asking them if you may). So I explained to the woman how I had happened to visit with her, and how she was not the person that I had intended on visiting, but how the visit had blessed me. (And I *was* telling the truth.)

At this point, she told me that although she didn't recognize me, she had just assumed that I had been the answer to her prayers, because she was all alone – with no family or friends or church folks having been to see her. I asked her if I could have permission to share – anonymously, of course – these facts, in order to tell people of how God surely does work in strange and mysterious ways. She agreed (which is why I'm able to share this story here) and then I prayed. As I recall it, I prayed not only for her well-being, but also a big "thank-you, God" for providing this unintended, and yet absolutely wonderful, serendipitous moment for both Mrs. __ and for me.

I like to be particularly observant from the moment I walk through the door. One of the things that I learned from doing hospital pastoral care work as part of the hospital staff[8] – when almost all of the visits are made to people whom

---

[8]   This was done in two different ways: (1) a CPE (clinical pastoral education) class as part of my seminary training, and (2) as a volunteer night call pastor, working twice a month from 11:00 pm until 7:00 am, responding to all calls for which a patient requested pastoral care and where pastoral care was written into the hospital protocol. This protocol included: (a) death or impending death; (b) when a patient is "coded" and the crash cart is called; (c) all cases of "trauma" brought in through the Emergency Room.

I would highly recommend both of these experiences for pastors. CPE teaches both the technical parts of hospital (and other) pastoral caregiving, as well as self-knowledge which is so important to being a good pastoral caregiver.

you've never met before and the circumstances are usually one of intensity -- is that there is a perceptible "aura" in the room.

I don't want you to throw down this book in disgust, that you have been tricked into reading a book by some new age, looking into crystals, kind of nut. Actually, I am none of those things. And I was rather taken aback when I finally began to realize what I had been noticing in these experi-

---

The volunteer night call ministry was very beneficial in a number of respects, including (a) when you are constantly being involved in "crisis" situations with people whom you don't have any prior knowledge, it reinforces the fundamental principle of pastoral care-giving that "you are not in charge; it's about God being in charge." There may come a time, after a while, when a pastor starts to get the notion that they are "good" at this pastoral caregiving. Pride goes before the fall! The night call ministry makes it impossible to ever believe that you are good. The circumstances are too overwhelming to ever feel like you know what to do. The circumstances drive you to prayer, over and over – with a real intense: ""Oh, God! What can I possibly do here? These people are devastated; I don't know their story, their history, their needs. What can I do? Help me here, God, *please!*" The repetition of this experience will go a long way in making this a habit, in your pastoral caregiving. And THIS is the only habit in which you ever want to take consolation at being "good" – knowing just how unworthy and unprepared and totally dependent on God's direction, just to get through it.

Such experience is also not a bad way to get familiar with the people who work in the hospital. Without expression of an opinion of its propriety, the hard reality of life is that people (like hospital work-ers) who know other people (like you, the pastor,) and who have been treated with respect by other people (like you, the pastor,) and who have seen other people (like you, the pastor,) work profession-ally and diligently and genuinely – will have a tendency, when they (like the hospital workers) encounter them (like you, the pastor,) to give them the benefit of the doubt, and will have a tendency to show them unconscious good will. And it sometimes might even mean that that pastor's parishioner could possibly get better care in the hospital! Good familiarity breeds respect and unconscious good will is one of the best tools to carry with you, when you enter the hospital. (Remember my granddaddy's advice: the quality of care people get in a hospital they carry in with them. You *can* plant that ahead of time, as well.)

ences, largely because the only words that came to mind to describe it – an "aura" – seemed to me to be just that: some new age, looking into crystals, kind of nuttiness.

But the hard reality I discovered is that *if* one pays careful attention when going into a room where there is an intensive life issue (including the life issue of impending death) being confronted, an observant person can detect a "something" that quickly tells you the spiritual/faith temperature in that room.

People of faith, for whom death or some impending large question mark situation is being encountered, exude a "something" that is perceptible. On the other hand, people for whom faith is a question mark (*irrespective of what their conduct or words express about their faith or religiosity*) who encounter the same kind of issue(s) will put off some different essence that an observant person can recognize. If you are familiar with the expression: "the atmosphere was so thick, you could cut it with a knife" – then you have a notion of what I'm describing.

In the Gospel of Thomas (Sayings)[9] Jesus is remembered to have said: ***Know what is in front of your face, and that which is hidden from you will be revealed unto you***. (5:1) This is a fundamental principle of spirituality, and also of pastoral caregiving. There are things which can be observed, which will reveal much – *even when* the expression of that which you observed will leave you trying to describe what goes beyond our normal vocabulary, and we end up using terms like "aura."

Pay attention to all of the little things. Surely, we are dependent upon God's guidance for how to respond effectively and meaningfully. But that does not mean that we are

---

[9] There are two Gospels of Thomas. The first, being the one quoted here, is distinguished from the other in title as: Gospel of Thomas (Sayings). It is a good text of these sayings of Jesus, written without narrative, much like a reading of the Sermon on the Mount / Plain. The other Gospel of Thomas is a fanciful set of narratives largely about Jesus' childhood. The former has been increasingly referred to in Biblical scholarship; the second, while interesting, has escaped much serious consideration for either its historicity nor its value other than for entertainment.

not to use all the faculties with which God gifted us, as tools of our ministry.

Certainly the principles of Chapter 5 (*It's Not About Me*) are applicable to the hospital setting as anywhere else. In the hospital, based on the condition of the patient, there may be need for you to do much more of the talking than in other pastoral care situations. That does not *necessarily* mean the talking will be about you.

As indicated in Chapter 5, it is acceptable, as "ice breaker" conversation to chit chat about what's going on in your life or the life of the Church. If the person is unable to speak at all, one of the gifts that you can bring to the person is news about good things going on in the life of the Church. (If you ever take this opportunity – regardless of how tempting it may be, particularly for someone now rendered speechless who tends to monopolize conversation or whom you've wanted to tell something but were afraid of how they would respond – to lay out a problem in the life of the Church, then you need to know that a special kind of punishment will be accorded you throughout all eternity! *Cf.* Matthew 12:36.)

Neither should you make comparative studies with this person about fellow parishioners who are also in the hospital, *e.g.* you certainly look a lot better than Mrs. So-and-so up on floor five. Only talk about other parishioners in the hospital (past or present) if this patient asks about their condition (and then only within the limits of confidentiality.)

There will be times – and it will be difficult for you, but not nearly so difficult as it is for them – when your parishioner will be intubated, but conscious and aware. They will want to speak. Tell them up front that you are aware that they can not, and should not, attempt to speak. Tell them that you are here to check on them, and to let them know that you and the Church care about them; but that you are not going to stay very long because you know how frustrating it must be to not be able to participate in the conversation.

If they are able, give them simple questions to which they can respond by a squeeze of your hand (after having asked them to squeeze your hand, to make sure that they are comfortably able to do so) or by some other non-verbal response (but only after you have pre-tested the response to see if they are able to do it.) The importance of this is to allow them to feel a sense of power, to overcome a sense of helplessness. But do not try to do a "regular" conversation this way. Never ask for more than a couple of such responses. It is too much work for them. They need rest. Your job is not to exercise them.

THE "SWEET SPOT"

In golf, there is a small spot on the face of the club (the part that makes contact with the ball) which is the exact spot where the weight and balance are perfect to make contact with the ball properly. This is called the "SWEET SPOT" of the club. Hitting the ball with some part of the club outside the sweet spot will cause a variety of things – none of them good. Most golfers spend their whole lives practicing trying to hit the ball with the sweet spot of the club a high percentage of the time.

The "SWEET SPOT" of pastoral caregiving – particularly in the hospital – is <u>15 minutes of being totally, absolutely, completely PRESENT WITH THE PATIENT</u>.

This "SWEET SPOT" is not something you can "fake." You need to set aside every single other thing that wants to run around through your mind

➢ your heavy work load,

➢ your concerns and fears for what the patient and/or the family are thinking of you as a pastor,

➢ your concerns and fears for whether this person is going to recover, or how well they are going to recover,

➢ what you are going to say in the prayer you offer up before you leave the room,

➢ and everything else

and be TOTALLY PRESENT with and to them.

Being "TOTALLY PRESENT" means that you are

➢ entirely focused on everything about them,

➢ looking for clues of their thoughts and emotions,

➢ paying attention to every word or idea they express – trying to test each for possible wrong interpretations that you could make, and sorting through them with questions to clarify, and

➤ trying to ascertain what are their fears or worries, (and, again, testing with gentle questions, so as to not make wrong assumptions).

Being "TOTALLY PRESENT" also means that you are present not merely as Rev'd So-and-so (or Pastor Such-and-such – whatever that person is comfortable calling you) It also means that you are present as the "Vicar of Christ" – the substitute physical presence for the Living and Resurrected Lord, Who arrived in the room prior to your coming. You are the flesh and blood physical presence that the patient can see, and hold onto with their hand. In order to do that, you must

➤ be praying the whole time for assistance in doing the above tasks of observation and testing,

➤ be working very hard to clear your body and mind and spirit of anything that would get in the way of Jesus' Presence being passed through you. I often try to picture my hand (which is appropriately firmly but gently holding the patient's hand) connected to my arm, to my shoulder, to my chest, which surrounds my heart – as though they are a hollow tube through which the Power of Jesus Himself courses and flows through to actually be passed through the flesh of my fingers and hands into the patient's body through their hand. Fixing on this image of "cleansing" the impurities and distractions and impediments in my "heart-to-hand" physical connection will result in cleansing more than just that portion of my body.

Why is the "SWEET SPOT" of pastoral care in the hospital "15 minutes of being totally, absolutely, completely PRESENT WITH THE PATIENT"? The answer is that it is extremely difficult to do it for more than 15 minutes straight.

It will wear you out!

You will need to take a break.

It will be the best gift you can give the person.

Varieties on the Theme

One of the delights of pastoral caregiving in the hospital is the rich variety you will discover. No two hospital visits (even to the same patient) will be the same. (If you find yourself getting into a routine (also known as "rut") of just following some formulaic ritual, then two things are happening:

1. You are not being real and genuine. This means that you are being as plastic as the plastic Jesus that taxi drivers in New York City have super glued to the dashboard of their taxis. Oh, the patient and/or the family will express appreciation (real or likewise plastic) and you can pat yourself on the back for having completed your task. And you may even find yourself (as a colleague in ministry told me his seminary professor once warned him) "good enough that you can fake it, and no one will know the difference." But "pretty, fake, plastic" is still plastic and fake,[10] which is never good pastoral care.

---

[10] I have to confess here to something that just bugs the bejeebers out of me. And it may, indeed, be just *my* problem. It's "THE PRAYER VOICE." THE PRAYER VOICE is that voice that somehow appears from nowhere, but now coming from the pastor's mouth when s/he prays, and it is wholly different from the voice that had been consistently heard in all conversation prior to that point. Some pastors have the same voice that also emanates as "THE PREACHING VOICE." It almost always is (for men) deeper and more resonant, like they are auditioning for the role of a radio announcer. It's not that it's an unpleasant voice, at all. In fact, sometimes, it is quite melodious. It's just that it's not the pastor's voice. The message that I hear whenever I hear "THE PRAYER VOICE" is that *God can't be approached by who we are* or that *I have to be someone other than who I really am in order to be able to talk to God.* It just doesn't seem like good theology in action. I am fully aware that some pastors are entirely unaware that they are doing it, and when asked about it, they "repent." I also know one pastor who "learned" in seminary that his "real voice" was "not good enough" and was taught how to intentionally modulate into "THE PRAYER VOICE." I only learned of this when one of his parishioners in a student appointment happened to hear him on another occasion, and mentioned to me something about how "he certainly puts on airs now."

2. And, you are not being "ᴛᴏᴛᴀʟʟʏ ᴘʀᴇsᴇɴᴛ" with the person – because being "ᴛᴏᴛᴀʟʟʏ ᴘʀᴇsᴇɴᴛ" means being real and genuine. To be real and genuine, while at the same time you are emptying yourself to make room for unencumbered flow of Jesus through you, may seem like a paradox. But, remember: ᴘᴀʀᴀᴅᴏx ɪs ᴏɴʟʏ ᴇxɪsᴛᴇɴᴛ ɪɴ ᴛʀʏɪɴɢ ᴛᴏ ᴘᴜᴛ ʀᴇᴀʟɪᴛʏ ɪɴᴛᴏ ᴡᴏʀᴅs ᴏʀ ᴄᴏɴᴄᴇᴘᴛs. Reality is that congruity which is experienced, regardless of the difficulty of its explanation. And the reality is that you cannot be "ᴛᴏᴛᴀʟʟʏ ᴘʀᴇsᴇɴᴛ" and let Jesus flow through you unencumbered, if you are not being real and genuine.

The varieties you discover in hospital visits are almost endless, in terms of the patient / parishioner's

1. levels of discomfort,
2. ability to communicate,
3. expressed and unexpressed fears and concerns about self and about how much bother it is for family and friends who carry the heavy load of watching, waiting, and picking up the slack at home or work
4. degree of crankiness and/or impatience (tends to increase over length of stay)
5. response to the variety of caregiving by doctors and hospital staff (both the timeliness/appropriateness of the physical care and the degree of compassion expressed by the staff while providing the physical care)
6. response to the limitations imposed
7. responses to visitation received from others
8. and the list goes on and on

Although I generally make it a practice to not give unsolicited advice in any pastoral caregiving (in the hospital or not), there are a few bits of "hospital wisdom" that I sometimes pass along, when appropriate:

➢ There are two things you, and every other patient in this hospital, left behind when you enter through those glass doors at the front of the hospital.

1. You left your modesty behind. It just won't work here. That's neither bad nor good; it's

        simply reality, and acceptance of that reality is helpful

2.   You left E.S.T. (Eastern Standard Time, or whatever is applicable in your place and season) and entered into H.S.T. That's Hospital Standard Time, and it's not the same as anywhere else in the universe. For example, when the nurse, doctor, etc. tells you that something will happen at 10:00 a.m., you may think s/he is referring to E.S.T. But 10:00 a.m. H.S.T. is almost always later than 10:00 a.m. E.S.T., and occasionally prior to 10:00 a.m. E.S.T., and almost never the same as 10:00 a.m. E.S.T. That's neither bad nor good; it's simply reality, and acceptance of that reality is helpful

➢ There is a reason to give thanks. Whatever the situation, there is always a reason to give thanks. I <u>never</u> say: "Well, God certainly has a plan for this." Nor: "Just look around you and you will see people worse off than yourself." (The first is trite; the second is condescending.) But there really <u>is</u> something good about which to give thanks in every circumstance. You don't want to come across as some flaming Pollyanna when you do this. The way to do this (has been my experience) is to <u>always</u> ask my hospital companion, Jesus, to give me some advice on what to say here.

➢ (Occasionally, I offer this advice:) My grandfather used to tell me, "The compassion and quality of care one receives in a hospital, they carry in with them when they walk through those doors."

That, my experience teaches me, <u>is</u> a reality. I have had some cranky patients (or, sometimes even more importantly, particularly if the patient is non-communicative, cranky family members) who seem to get cranky inferior care wherever they are a patient – regardless of which hospital, unit, or nurses' station. And yet, grateful, appreciative patients (and families) tend to receive timely, appropriate, compassionate care from the very same hospital personnel.

I had a parishioner who was, unfortunately, a "frequent flyer" in hospitals during his last years. He always had his wife bring in a large box of assorted chocolates (Russell Stover, etc.) which he opened up and put on the hospital tray stand. He always told the nurses that he didn't like chocolates; but these were for them. That guy always had lots of loving attention given him by all the nurses. (I suspect that this attention was due to the fact that he thought about them, as opposed to a tawdry "being bought with chocolate.")

One time, as I shared that story with another parishioner, he said simply, "I don't need chocolates." I said something noncommittal, as he was at that very moment going through a really cranky period with his family, whom he though was not giving him appropriate attention. However, as soon as a nurse walked in to check on him, this man demonstrated to me what he meant. The put-upon-woe-is-me patient suddenly transformed into a kindly, grandfatherly type, solicitous of the well being of this kind-sister-of-mercy-who-came-to-minister-to-his-needs. It was uncanny to see the instant metamorphosis in the man. After she left the room, he turned to me, smiled, and repeated: "See, I don't need chocolate." But it was clear that he understood the principle: "The compassion and quality of care one receives in a hospital, they carry in with them when they walk through those doors."

I do not ever pass along this advice when it seems like I am being "preachy" to some crank. If that is the atmosphere in the room, I will never pass it along, unless there might be some break in the ice in which the patient does express some kindness, which I can reasonably reinforce. I have less compunction against being "preachy" with cranky family of a non-communicative patient, since their attitude can very well impact the quality of care their loved one is going to receive.

Two Absolutes

I need to highlight two aspects of the hospital visit, that usually occur near the end of the visit.

<u>One</u>: I never, <u>never</u>, <u>never</u> tell the person (or their family) <u>WHEN</u> I will be back to visit. It doesn't matter what may be my very best intentions. The pure and simple reality of the life of a pastor is that, other than Sunday worship and a set time for a funeral or a wedding, there is almost nothing that we can guarantee we will be able to attend at a time certain. (Well, OK, maybe charge conference or an appointment with the District Superintendent or Bishop.) The reason is very simple: Stuff happens! And as important as hospital visitation may be, (a) someone may die in the interim [death and funeral ministry "trumps" hospital visitation – as well as just about everything else in ministry]; (b) an emergency develops in the building – with the building, with a drop-in crisis, with a whole host of other things.

I almost always tell the person something along the lines of "I'll see you again" when I leave. Even, if I'm not sure if they will still be alive when I return, I <u>will</u> plan on seeing them again – on the other side.

(Do I also say this, if I'm not at all convinced that this person will inhabit the same place for eternity where I'm planning on going? Yes, for the reasons explained in Chapter 13, that can be briefly stated as:

Ashes to ashes, dust to dust,
if God doesn't get them,
then the devil must!

I ought not make any assumptions about their having a different forwarding address than I will.)

Here's the reason why you <u>don't say when</u> you will be back to visit:

We (each and every one of us) apply a double standard for our lives:

➢ ***I judge other people by their actions,***
➢ ***but I expect other people to judge me by my intentions***

When someone promises me that they will do something, and then they fail to do it, that failure is the first thing that registers in my database under the file with their name on it. Oh, I may also make a note of the fact that this person had a good (or not so good) excuse. But the first thing I note, and remember, is that this person let me down. With not even very much repetition of such behavior – regardless of how good the excuse was each time – that person's file (in the filing cabinet or computer data base that lives in my head) now has a label on it next to their name that says something like: "undependable" or "unreliable." It is the conduct of the other person that registers.

However, when I fall short, and am unable to keep some appointment, the primary thing that registers in my brain about my own conduct is (a) I had good intentions, and (b) I had a good reason for not keeping my appointment. That combination tends to outweigh any notion of my failure of conduct. And I certainly do not keep the same kind of running tab for myself that I do for other people.

We need to understand, too, that people will appear to be gracious and to accept our "excuse/reason" but are indeed (consciously or unconsciously) developing a file of non-credibility or untrustworthiness about me, and I don't even know it.

So I never give a time certain when I will be back.

Once upon a time, a mother of one of my parishioners had an extended post-surgical hospital admission. I periodically spent time at the hospital visiting the mother, when the daughter parishioner was also there. During one of those visits, the mother/patient's pastor also came. He was a friend of mine, and there was no discomfort at all with us both being there.

Not too long after that, I got a call from my parishioner telling me that her mother had died, and the family wanted me to do the funeral. I was a bit hesitant, and made inquiries about her mother's own pastor. I was told in no uncertain terms that the family did not want him to do the funeral.

Prior to her death, I had (just in passing) talked to Mom's pastor about how she was doing. It was quite plain to me that he had been keeping good contact with the mother in the hospital, and with the family. So I wasn't really sure what was going on. Later on, during public visitationat the funeral home, I overheard from some of the family discussing what the issue had been: Two days before her death, the mother's pastor had said that he would be back the next day. Something came up and he did not make it back that "next day," and she died the following day, before he arrived at the hospital. They referred to him as "that lying preacher."

Although he had provided good and regular pastoral care, he had missed a "day certain" appointment. Particularly in the angst that accompanies death, the previous pastoral care was all seemingly forgotten; all that stood out was the failure of the pastor to keep that one appointment. He became "that lying preacher."

I don't fault the family; grief often causes thinking to become unclear, and focused inappropriately on just one thing. And the pastor was himself quite new – still a rookie – and no one had ever told him about this lesson.

When you leave the hospital, particularly if the person is not doing very well, there is an intense pressure to say "when" you will come back. And in that moment, you will also feel a pressure to state a time that you would really like to come back, even if it's not at all reasonable. It just doesn't sound right to say "when" you're coming back, if it's not very, very soon. Away from the hospital, and the other pressures of the job come to the forefront, and you are being TOTALLY PRESENT with someone else, it is easy to forget – or, just as bad – to rationalize that you had good intentions and a good excuse, as though this is good enough.

Avoid that pressure. Avoid setting yourself up for letting others down. Avoid setting yourself up to damage your ministry. Whenever you leave, <u>never</u>, <u>never</u> tell the person (or their family) <u>WHEN</u> you will be back to visit.

<u>Absolute number 2</u> Always have prayer. It's what they pay you to do. It's what you are – your most important identity: a person of prayer. It is what you should do best, based on the practices you keep. It is what your people need more than anything from the Doctor of their Soul.

Unless ... (an absolute with an unless??)

Yes, unless, it seems to you that the person has only tolerated your presence and would be put off by prayer. In such cases where I do not pray for the person in their presence, I always pray for them when I leave the room. It's not about performance on a stage; it's about what I am paid to do; about my identity as a Doctor of the Soul, as a person of prayer.

These "unless" cases are usually pretty rare. They have come up for me sometimes when I was doing hospital chaplaincy work, or when I am visiting with an unchurched family member of one of my parishioners (whom they oftentimes want me to "save" before it's too late.) It's not a difficult dilemma to handle. If I sense an uneasiness on their part, I simply ask, "Would it be alright if I had prayer with you before I leave?" And, with very few exceptions, I am always given permission, if not blessing to do so.

On a couple of occasions, the person has told me that they would rather I not. But each time afterwards when I visited, I always asked the same thing. Usually, after they are comfortable with the notion that I am there to love them – not to "fix" them – they are comfortable being a listening participant in a conversation between my Friend, Jesus, and me.

There was one occasion – was I very tired or what? – when I had a very strong sense of discomfort between the patient (non-attending child of a parishioner) whose chosen lifestyle was not one endorsed by many orthodox churchgoers. He was a beloved child of God, in my eyes, and I did all I could while I was there to let him know that this was my opinion. But I didn't feel like I was getting through. I felt like I was putting him into a great discomfort zone. So instead of asking Jesus what to do; instead of asking him if he minded if I prayed, I simply bid him well and adieu.

Not long after that, the parishioner made a passing comment that her son thought it seemed very peculiar that her preacher had not prayed with him before he left.

So I did what I have made my practice – particularly when I mess up – I told her the truth, including why I had not prayed in the room with him, and that I had done so, once I got out of the room. She understood (or so she said, and I tended to think she meant it.)

And I learned my lesson. Always pray!

There are a few additional thoughts about hospital visitation *for the family* of the patient. They have a different set of pastoral care needs. Over the first decade of my pastoral ministry I conducted an unscientific poll. Whenever

I thought of it, I asked everyone – who had been both a patient and one who waited with a patient – which was the harder task. I didn't write down the answers; I didn't need to. With *only one exception*, everyone who had had experience with both said that being the patient was easier than being the one who watched and waited.

At least, during surgery, the patient gets to go to sleep.

Please don't get me wrong; it's no fun and games being a patient, but the needs of the caregivers are quite real, as well.

A question arises as to how long the pastor should stay with the family that waits during surgery. In my earlier days of pastoral ministry, when the congregations (and their corporate needs) were smaller, I always stayed with the family for the duration of the surgery. Larger congregations don't diminish the needs of the family, but do diminish one person's ability to give as much to each person.

Right now, I try to make sure that I am always there with the patient and the family before the surgery begins – to have prayer with them all. I usually remind the patient that anesthesia has a strange effect, in that the thought that is on their mind when they go to sleep will be the same thought when they awaken. If you "go out" while speaking, and are mid-sentence, you will complete the sentence, when you awaken. So I tell them to be focused on their favorite vacation spot when they go to sleep, so that's where their mind will be when they awaken.

How long I stay with the family after the patient goes to surgery depends on a wide variety of circumstances:

➢ The seriousness / danger of the surgery

➢ How well the family is coping with the stress

➢ Alas, how busy is the schedule of other needs calling for me on that day

➢ Most importantly, what I discern through prayer, that God directs me to do

Once, one of my parishioners had surgery, that did not seem all that risky. I had visited with him and his family at home the week before. After we had prayer and I went with the family to the waiting area, I stayed for just a bit. Children who now lived out of state had come home. (That is one opportunity for the pastor: in the hospital waiting area is where you can sometimes best get to know the family.)

On the surface, there was not a real need for me to stay much longer. In fact, on that day, I was feeling like I was coming down with some sort of "bug," and I planned on leaving shortly and going home to bed. But, that little voice inside, that nudges my pastoral instincts, told me to "hold on." And so I stayed throughout the successful surgery.

As sometimes happens, however, (and the odds jump a lot with each decade over 65) the surgery was a complete success, but the patient died. It was not immediate, and it came as a great surprise to everyone. I later learned, during time at the funeral home, that at the time of surgery, one of the daughters had been miffed with me – for interfering with their privacy in staying at the hospital so long. (That *is* a very real risk for many families.) However, as her daddy deteriorated and then passed through that doorway we call "death," she realized that my presence on that day had not been an intrusion, at all, but was, a real blessing, which she now realized she needed.

There are no hard fast rules for this. The best I can say is that the pastor needs to pay close attention to all the clues about the family's needs, and needs to be very much in tune with the direction that God gives.

There are a few rules that are good to follow, just about all the time. Your knowledge of the simple geography of the hospital is enormously helpful. We pastors tend to get as used to maneuvering through those mammoth structures, as does the hospital staff. Try to remember the first time you went into that facility, and how unfriendly it was. Simple direction giving can lower a lot of stress.

One of the more common, and serious, surgeries is open heart / bypass surgery (although it is actually not very dangerous anymore, in good hospitals.) The "normal" condition of the patient after a successful operation is a tremendous shock to someone who has not seen it before. When first visited, after surgery, the patient's skin color is about the same pale color as funeral home powder. There are lines and tubes and machines and distortion of features that makes the loved one look grotesque and *very scary*. I have found that if I tell a spouse, child, close relative when we go back to that recovery room that their loved one's appearance is "normal," it does not have near the same credibility as if I tell them ahead of time what to expect. Families have, afterwards, thanked me a lot for that warning.

One of the other important things I have learned for those times sitting in the waiting room is the value of silence. As a culture, we have a penchant to avoid silence at all costs. Time in a waiting area can be long and arduous. The family should not feel like they have to be a constant conversation partner. Don't feel like you have to fill the air with your voice.

I remember one time when my wife went into hospital for a surgical procedure. A member of our Church, who worked in the medical profession, decided to come and be a pastor to the pastor and family. The intent was greatly appreciated. But he had a hard time with silence. And he felt like he had to give us the benefit of his experience in the hospital. So, for the better part of an hour, he sat with us and shared lots of "hospital stories," some of which were of people who died from the procedure my wife was about to have, and some of which were "insider" hospital stories. In another setting, some might have been humorous, but under the circumstances they did very little to inspire our confidence in the people who were going to come out and put my wife under.

Keep your prayer book, or Bible, as a companion when you go to hospital. Occupy some of your quiet ministry of presence with the family, by being in prayer. It's not about appearance; it's about being who you are – a person of prayer.

PRAYER

[C. S. "Jack" Lewis:] "Good news, I think. Yes, good news." [about the cancer of his wife, Joy]

"I'm very glad, Jack," smiled Riley. Even the severe portraits of former presidents and celebrated scholars hanging in their gilded frames on the wood-paneled walls [of Magdalen College, Oxford] seemed to be smiling.

"Christopher can scoff," said [the Rev'd Harry] Harrington, "but I know how hard you've been praying, Jack. And now God is answering your prayer."

Lewis smoothed out the creases in his gown and took his place in the forming line. He spoke very seriously, **"That's not why I pray, Harry. I pray because I can't help myself. I pray because I'm helpless. I pray because the need flows out of me all the time, waking and sleeping. It doesn't change God. It changes me."**

"There's your answer, Christopher," laughed Rupert Parrish.

"That's the first sensible thing I've ever heard anybody say on the subject," ceded Riley [the atheist].

7
LISTENING AND TRUST BUILDING

Eternal God, our beginning and our end,
be our starting point and our haven,
and accompany us in this day's journey.
Use our hands to do the work of your creation,
and use our lives to bring others
the new life you give this word,
in Jesus Christ, Redeemer of all. Amen.

Book of Common Worship,
Presbyterian Church USA & Cumberland Presbyterian Church

In the only "conflict resolution" advice specifically given by Jesus,

> [15]"If another member of the church sins against you, go and point out the fault when the two of you are alone. If the member listens to you, you have regained that one. [16]But if you are not listened to, take one or two others along with you, so that every word may be confirmed by the evidence of two or three witnesses. [17]If the member refuses to listen to them, tell it to the church; and if the offender refuses to listen even to the church, let such a one be to you as a Gentile and a tax collector. (Matthew 18)

He makes the "TEST FOR SUCCESS" a very simple one (although not always read as such.) The test for resolution of

75

the conflict is <u>not</u> whether you get the one who offends you to change. The test is merely *IF HE LISTENS*.

<u>LISTENING</u> is the foundation of life in community, of life together in the Body of Christ.

One of the basic, most often unfulfilled needs of the human creature, is the need for people to be heard and understood.

How important is this? Don't we all feel like we have something important to say? Don't we all want someone to listen to what we think is important?

But it's a rare experience for most of us (unless, you happen to have a job where you get to stand up in the pulpit every Sunday morning.) And I'm not talking here about everybody wants to get up in a pulpit – not everyone wants to get up on any kind of soap box and do public speaking. (Actually, the surveys say that is the biggest fear in America – more than fear of flying, fear of getting cancer, any of them – it's the fear of public speaking.) So, that's not what we are talking about here.

Rather we are dealing with the great need people have for someone to actually take time to listen to them – and to listen for the purpose of hearing.

How many people do this? How many people REALLY listen, with a desire to pay attention and to understand? Roy Trueblood[11] says that these people are so rare that when we meet someone like that, they either become our best friend or we marry them.

Can you count how many people in your life are like that?

What we as Christians need to do is to develop the skills of really listening to people <u>and to give them evidence that we are listening to them</u>. We may not FULLY understand them, and people understand that. But it means a tremendous amount if they know that we are trying.

Some mental health counselors say that a large percentage of people who come to them for professional ser-

---

[11] For many of the principles incorporated in this chapter the author is indebted to Roy Trueblood, who trained the author as a facilitator in a wonderful congregational instructional event called *Partners in Ministry*

vices could be helped just as much if they had a GOOD FRIEND – someone who would listen to them NON-JUDG-MENTALLY AND TRY TO UNDERSTAND

Jesus was like that, you know. *What a Friend We Have in Jesus.* The Gospels tell us over and over how He did this. And He still does it today. But if we want people to be introduced to that Friend, they need to come through us. And we need to develop the skills so that we can draw people, by learning how to listen to them non-judgmentally, and by trying to understand them.

Doesn't it make you feel good when people listen to you? Don't you want to be around them? People didn't come to Jesus just to hear what He had to say – but also because this WONDERFUL COUNSELOR listened to them.

LISTENING. It seems so easy. Yet much of what we do is poorly done.

We are creatures of habit, and have gotten content in our LISTENING SLOTH.

But don't feel too badly – you haven't had much of a chance. In school, you were taught to read, write, and speak. But unless you are a special professional (e.g. psychologist, counselor, salesperson) you have maybe never had any training in listening.

Listening is the cornerstone of pastoral caregiving. It

> Demonstrates CARING and GENUINE CONCERN
> Enables you to understand another person's frame of reference and needs
> Allows you to get important information
> Enables you to influence others and to impact situations.

Listening, really, is not very difficult – BUT it does RE-QUIRE CONSCIOUS ATTENTION. And that often is HARD WORK. One of the real shocks to me when I entered pastoral ministry was how totally exhausted I found myself at the end of the day, when the only thing I had been doing was "just listening" to people all day.

Initially, we need to note just how many things tend to distract us from listening.

> Other thoughts running through our head
> The last person we were just with

> ➢ The next person we are going to see
> ➢ The history that we have with the person to whom we are listening right now
> ➢ Anything distracting about the person to whom we are listening (at least three of the five senses come into play here: sight, sound, smell)
> ➢ The "agenda" that we think we want to accomplish in the time spent with this person
> ➢ And the list can go on and on.

Be aware of natural distractions. This is more than half of the battle – to recognize and name the "demons" is to take power away from them. (That principle is true not just for distractions in listening!)

One of the other barriers to listening is when the person we want to listen to has a certain hesitancy – they may come to you for help, and yet, at the same time, do not want to be "put down." (Too often, alas, the Church and her pastors are perceived as "agents of guilt and put down.") Breaking down that barrier requires your letting the person know that you are not there to "make them wrong."

Most of us have had the experience in life of being put down by someone – and in front of others. How does that feel? It hurts, doesn't it? It really hurts!

Our response to that is often: SMILE, BUT I'M GOING TO GET YOU BACK or O.K. FINE. BUT I'LL NEVER HAVE ANYTHING TO DO WITH YOU AGAIN.

We are NOT ATTRACTED to put down artists – to people who make us wrong. We ARE attracted to people who have different opinions, but who respect us, and who respect our differences.

Now, wouldn't you think – based on how strong our feelings are about these put down – wouldn't you think that the one place that we wouldn't have such behavior would be in the church? But guess what? Yep.

Please hear me correctly. I'm not saying here that we have to agree with everyone. What I AM saying is that we CAN disagree. But we don't have to step over the line from that and make the other person wrong. It's such a THIN LINE which gets crossed so imperceptibly, between "YOUR IDEA IS WRONG" and **"YOU ARE WRONG."**

Q: When people do this to you, what's your natural response? A: You get defensive. (right?) And then polarities develop. And instead of being bound together in Christ, we are pushing one another away. We become the church of the outstretched hands ... but instead of the palms being up and inviting, they are pushing away.

Do we have any issues in the Church today where people have taken differences of opinions and have begun to MAKE LABELS for people who have differing opinions? We move beyond the difference of opinion into the realm of personal attack – which is all a label is, after all.

As Christians, surely we should be able to separate the person from the opinion, or the life style. The Apostle Paul told the Church at Ephesus – our enemies are not of flesh and blood. (Ephesians 6:12)

A recent commentator on Jesus said that his commandment "Love your enemy" is impossible – because when you love your enemy (the person), that person is no longer your enemy.

Do you remember the story about Jesus and the woman caught in the act of adultery, from the 8th chapter of John? The Pharisees dragged her before Jesus – because they were always into playing the Win / Lose game with Jesus. And do you remember how Jesus dealt with the woman – after the rest of them went away. He told her two things: (1) **Go and sin no more.** Jesus knew what sin was. And this woman had been doing it – this person that Jesus loved had done things with which Jesus disagreed. (2) But what was the other thing that He said? **Neither do I condemn YOU.**

Jesus separated <u>her</u> from the sin.

I don't know anyone who has been won over to Jesus Christ by being beaten over the head by elegant theology. If you're a Christian today, I'm guessing that it's because some one approached you in love and demonstrated that they cared about you.

One way that we can give our conversation partner an assurance that we're not out to "make <u>them</u> wrong," is to offer to them signs that we recognize the unique value that each one has as a beloved child of God, precious and beautiful to behold.

79

It's a skill that Jesus exemplified in His ministry. What did He do with Simon? Saw the Rock of Strength upon which the Church would be built and gave him a new name. How about Nathanael? (You remember His first encounter with old "what-good-could-can-come-out-of-Nazareth" Nathanael.) Jesus understood Nathanael's hesitancy, but rather than arguing with him, he told Nathanael that he (Nathanael) was a person without guile. And how did Nathanael respond?

Jesus was probably the best at this of all that He did. He was able to hold a mirror up to people so that they could see the good that was in them – to see their potential – potential that they could not even see themselves. He showed them the Image in which they were made, and encouraged them to live up to that potential.

I don't think people were following Jesus around because He was beating them over the head and telling them what a bunch of losers they were. Instead, they followed Him because He saw something in them, and told them about it – something that no one else had ever acted like they even noticed.

Not only should we look for the unique goodness in each person we meet, and let them see it, but we also look for the good intentions of each person.

In all the years that I prosecuted people for breaking the law, I came across very, very, very few (I could count them on the fingers of one hand) people who would wake up each morning, asking the question, "What evil can I do today?" **Everyone lives out of their own story, and what they do makes sense to them, based on that story**.[12]

---

[12] We may not understand that story, without careful listening and investigation – and sometimes, even then, it's very difficult. And, certainly, not all people, including the author and perhaps the reader of this text, always do what they know to be the right thing. We surely are all sinners, in need of grace. But we really do have a tendency to "hair trigger" bad motives simply when we don't agree with the conduct. That's why God reserves solely to God's portfolio the right to judge people. We simply can't know what goes on in people's hearts, and all the circumstances of their story that led them to make the decisions they do. It's amazing, isn't it, with all of the tasks the Lord God has given us to do, and how God reserves just that one – "judgment" – and we are all over doing that one we're not supposed to touch, while leaving so many other tasks we *are* supposed to do, untouched.

How often every single one of us has had good intentions, but sometimes good results didn't follow. Have you ever worked on something really hard, and it flopped? When those results lead me to beat up on myself, the last thing I need is for someone else to "pile on." What I could really use would be someone coming up and saying, "Geez, Monty, I know you worked really hard on this, and this sure isn't how you thought it was going to turn out. But I recognize how much you tried."

It doesn't take away all the hurt, but it sure does help. And it surely feels a lot better than:

"Boy that was a loser of a project wasn't it, Monty? What in the world were you thinking about when you started? I knew all along that it was a loser. How did you ever sell it to the Board to go along with it?"

Number 1 or Number 2? Not much of a choice, is it? But you've had people do #2, haven't you? How often have you had #1?

Do you remember the way everyone piled on the woman who wasted all the expensive oil on Jesus' feet? How did Jesus respond? He looked for her good intentions. And He found them. And not only did He find them, but He lifted them up, saying that whenever the good news is told, this story would be included. And, sure enough, all four Gospels contain this one story – one of the few events, besides the crucifixion and resurrection, that is in all four.

All of these ways of looking at, and communicating with, people not only free you (the listener) from distractions that prevent your hearing them, but they also will free them (the speaker) to be more open in expressing themselves to you. It makes for good pastoral caregiving.

THE PASTORAL TRUST RELATIONSHIP

In chapter 6 (*In the Hospital Room*) we looked at how you should never give a "time certain" when you are going to make a return visit, for the reason that broken promises lead to resentment and feelings of the pastor being untrustworthy.

Being trusted is fundamental to being a good pastoral caregiver.

The most important area in which trust can be built (over time) and destroyed (instantly) is the matter of KEEPING CONFIDENCES. There is no more sacred obligation of the pastor than that of keeping quiet about what has been told in confidence.

What is told "in confidence?"

The general rule of thumb is ANYTHING SPOKEN TO THE PASTOR WHEN JUST THE PASTOR AND THE PERSON SPEAKING ARE ALONE.

It's not so much the *subject matter* that makes it confidential as it is the intent of the person giving the information.

How can you determine what their intent is?

Good question. It's almost impossible. So, unless they say it in front of other people (thus making it not confidential in its speaking) then the only safe way to handle it is to keep it quiet yourself.

Period.

No exceptions, unless you specifically ask for permission to share the information, and that permission is given.[13]

It is impossible to state just how much damage the violation of the Trust of Confidentiality does. It is not just damage to the person violated. It is not just damage to the pastor who violated the parishioner. It does damage, for as far as the ripples of this gross violation of pastoral identity spread across the water of the Church. I'm certain that I cannot explain just how much damage control and work I have had to attempt in trying to bring people back to the Church and to Jesus – all because of a pastor who violated the sacred trust of confidentiality.

Keep it simple.

Keep it black and white.

---

[13] There is just one exception, and that is where the Discipline (or polity book of your denomination) authorizes or directs it. For example, our Bishop recently sent all clergy the written direction from the chancellor of the West Virginia Annual Conference about the exception that is required in cases of child abuse and neglect which is shared with a pastor in what may be seen as a confidential setting. Clergy are required to divulge / report this information.

ANYTHING SPOKEN TO THE PASTOR -- WHEN JUST THE PASTOR AND THE PERSON SPEAKING ARE ALONE -- IS CONFIDENTIAL AND CANNOT BE SPOKEN BY YOU TO <u>ANYONE</u> WITHOUT THE SPECIFIC AUTHORIZATION OF THE PERSON WHO TOLD YOU. THIS IS <u>IRRESPECTIVE</u> OF WHAT GREATER GOOD YOU MIGHT IMAGINE WOULD BE SERVED.

Having addressed this cornerstone trust which is part of the definition of pastoral identity and integrity, let us turn to some of the other trust issues that define pastoral caregiving.

Trust is a really strange thing, in that people rarely (if ever) have any control over how they form and break down "who they trust." One of the most precious parts of being a pastor is the "built-in" trust factor that goes with the job. (Believe it or not, I have an easier time saying, and having believed: "Trust me, I'm a pastor," than I did with "Trust me, I'm a lawyer.") People, on the whole, really do trust pastors, and turn to pastors in the moments of most intense emotions in their lives.

People "on the whole" do. But not everyone, particularly people who have been wounded by the Church, by a previous pastor, or, perhaps, even by you.

Trust just seems to be formed or broken down without conscious thought. You simply cannot talk yourself into trusting someone. The old saying, "It has to be earned" has a lot of truth.

Strange as it may sound, however, even though Trust cannot be artificially generated by the person doing the trusting, it <u>can</u> be intentionally generated by the person seeking to be trusted. And, given the right stimulus, the other person is almost incapable to not allowing that trust to build.

The formula is very simple. Repetition of agreements made and kept builds trust.

Let me repeat this simple formula: Repetition of agreements made and kept builds trust.

It really is just a reverse of the way that credibility is broken down (as discussed in chapter 6.) And the fascinating aspect of this formula is that it is the *number* of agreements, more than the *size* of the agreement that is controlling.

If there is someone who has a trust problem with you (for whatever reason: general distrust of clergy, dislike of the Church, having been "stood up" by your not keeping agreements in the past [remember your intent + excuse validity have nothing to do with it!]) then the surest way to build that trust level up is to make lots of agreements and absolutely keep them.

Again, it is the number of repetitions, rather than the size of the agreements, that is determinative.

Make a conscious, intentional effort to make lots of "little agreements" with the person. For example,

> ➢ I will call you this week
> ➢ I will find this for you this week
> ➢ I will ask for your opinion on this project
> ➢ I will ….[whatever]

And when you make this promise, you had better make sure that you keep it. Over time, the person with whom you have made the agreements will literally be almost totally unable to control the fact that their trust in you has increased – even if they had been pretty content in nursing their discontent about clergy in general, the Church in general, or you in particular. They just won't be able to help the fact that they trust you more and more. (If the initial problem is one of your own personal making, this person may still not "like" you, but will nonetheless trust you. And sometimes, trusting leads to acceptance, which may – in a time of need – even lead to appreciation or the beginnings of liking.)

Of course, it may not need to be stated, but probably deserves to be: **the key in this "breaking" (happens fairly quickly) and "making" (usually takes longer) trust is how "agreements" are actually made.**

If you make an agreement with someone to do something, but you intentionally make that agreement "fuzzy," so as to allow you some "wiggle room," you are setting yourself up for failure. Lawyers are paid to make agreements so that their clients have lots of "wiggle room," in case their clients need to "wiggle" without being held liable for breach of contract. The other party to the contract may not like it, but the "fuzziness" of definitions used allows the "wiggler" to get away with it.

As a pastor, you are not an attorney. You may make a simple agreement fuzzy enough that in the courtroom of your own mind, you did not violate the agreement. However, in the courtroom of expectations that lives solely in the head and heart of the other person – where verdicts of "Trustworthiness" are involuntarily made, you can still be found "Guilty" or "Untrustworthy." Those verdicts are solely within the auspices of the other person, regardless of how you may feel you have "justifiably wiggled."

Jesus said, "Let your 'yes' be 'yes,' and your 'no' be 'no.'" It's good advice. Talk simply. Don't make promises (agreements) based on what you'd *like to be able to do*; but make only agreements that you have good confidence you *will* be able to keep.

Listening and Trustworthiness are not just the stock and trade of the pastor. They are precious gifts given us, to be treasured and protected – for your sake, personally, and for the whole Body of Christ.

```
┌─────────────────────────────────────────┐
│  ┌───────────────────────────────────┐  │
│  │              A Nugget             │  │
│  └───────────────────────────────────┘  │
└─────────────────────────────────────────┘
```

PERSON OF PRAYER

During a midweek Bible study, the students were discussing how to pray. The teacher passed out slips of paper, and asked each person to write down whom they would ask to teach them how to pray.

The responses were varied, with several persons identified by name. A few of them said, "My pastor." And a few said, "My Sunday School teacher."

But one response summarized what was perhaps intended by all of the responses:

If I wanted to learn how to pray, I would ask a PERSON OF PRAYER.

This is what the Pastor is getting paid to do, to be: a PERSON OF PRAYER. It is our identity, our calling, our specialty … and, too often, that which gets bumped to the bottom of our "to do list" by much busy work of the office of pastor.

I've never seen an orchestra tune their instruments, after the concert. Start your day with prayer.

Don't forget. The flock is depending on you. Practice what you are – a PERSON OF PRAYER.

87

8
SACRAMENTAL PASTORAL CARE

We are not worthy, O Lord, so as to gather the crumbs from under Your table, but say the Word, and we shall be healed.

The sacraments are a powerful part of worship. The United Methodist Church has recently adopted two important foundational documents on them: *This Holy Mystery* (adopted at 2004 General Conference as to Holy Communion) which can and absolutely should be read at

http://www.gbod.org/worship/default.asp?act=reader&item_id=4814)

and *By Water and the Spirit* (adopted at 1996 General Conference as to Baptism) which can and absolutely should be read at

http://www.gbod.org/worship/images/water&spirit.pdf

Chapter 4 (*Because … Therefore*) has already laid out some of the impact that Baptism can, and should, have on our pastoral caregiving. Another story, told by one of West Virginia's finest pastors (Heather Murray Elkins, of Drew Divinity School) illustrates how this works:

There had been a retreat where a group of preachers gathered to think, talk, and learn about Baptism. For their closing exercise, they each took their turn explaining the Baptismal Name that they claimed as their authority to teach and preach.

It went fine -- each person sharing what they had gained from their three days together; until -- one young pastor threw a fly into the ointment of good feeling that was present. At his turn, he came forward and sat down.

Everyone waited. SILENCE.

Everyone waited MORE SILENCE.

They were starting to get impatient, like most Christians today get impatient when SILENCE BEGINS TO EXPRESS ITSELF.

Chairs began to creak; throats were cleared; watches were consulted around the circle.

Finally the young man shifted his gaze from his hands to some spot above their heads.

I've been looking for my name for three days. But it's not there.

What did he mean,   *Not there*??

It's not that I don't want one of those wonderful names I have heard you claim. The problem is that they just aren't strong enough.   **PAUSE**   *There's none strong enough to* **undo the one I already have. My father gave it to me. OVER AND OVER.** *My name is ...* his gaze shifted down to his fingers.

My name is **NOT GOOD ENOUGH.**

There was a deep silence -- deep enough to drown in. Tears began to rise.

All the ministers present sat and looked on helplessly from the shoreline of this river of grief -- this confession of inadequacy. In a room full of lifeguards, this minister had revealed that he was drowning.

Then there came a stir -- as one, then two, then three, and then more men and women rose from their chairs and moved over to form a circle around him -- and they touched him. Without realizing, perhaps, that they were performing a Remembrance of Baptism, one voice said simply **YOU ARE MY BELOVED SON. WITH YOU I AM WELL PLEASED**. And then they all joined in unison to repeat these words that Jesus made possible for each baptized person to hear in their own ears. **YOU ARE MY BELOVED CHILD. WITH YOU I AM WELL PLEASED**.

What they witnessed in this unplanned sacramental moment was a rebirth. Afterwards, Heather asked the man, *What difference will this make?*

I don't know.   Something -- and he touched his chest -- *something in here that was broken is fixed. Now, whenever I put my hand in the water, I will remember*.

Our other Sacrament, Holy Communion, also has powerful impact on pastoral caregiving. I read in a study once, in which the lopsided balance between the responses did not surprise me:

If the doctor told you that you had two weeks to live, which would you want:

(a) to hear a sermon _____

(b) to receive Holy Communion _____

Answer (b) was overwhelmingly chosen.

Part of what we need for Holy Communion to work powerfully among our people is a "getting over" the notion that it is merely a "remembrance" ritual. It is that, but oh so much more.

Holy Communion is a sacred memory of Jesus' final meal with his Apostles prior to the Passion, Crucifixion and Resurrection. The Apostles didn't understand it then, but when they looked back on it, they were able to see what it was all about.

Part of the Great Thanksgiving liturgy for Holy Communion says, "**Do this in remembrance of Me**."

In the tenth book of his *Confessions*, St. Augustine discusses memory:

That great harbour of the memory receive[s] in her numberless secret and inexpressible windings, to be forthcoming and brought out at need; each entering in by his own gate, and there laid up. Nor yet do the things themselves enter in; only the images

91

of the things perceived are there in readiness, for thought to recall.

It is indeed amazing that this elder statesman of the Church, could 1500 years before the birth of Sigmund Freud, have such keen insights into what we now call psychology. For he was so correct. Actual events do not enter and live in our memory; only our perception of events resides in our memory. Augustine hit on what few of us realize: the past can be changed for us. How we hold the past in the treasure trove of our memory is indeed "the past" for us.

And Jesus, that greatest of psychologists (no surprise, since He created all of the parts involved) was able to give these first disciples a gift which would change the pain and sorrow of His Passion and Crucifixion into something beautiful. By the Gift of this Memorial Service of the Last Supper, something ugly and terrible was transformed into something exquisite. **Do this in remembrance of Me.** Convert the sinfulness of moralistic mishandlers of human power unto death, and your own paralyzing guilt, into a gift of My tender compassion – in your memory. Do this as often as you eat and drink it, in remembrance of Me.

Have you ever heard the term "**Comfort Food**"? Comfort Food is the meal that your mother brought to you when you were sick as a child. For me, it's Tomato Soup and Egg Salad Sandwiches. Can you remember a Comfort Food in your past? And, now -- even today -- when you eat that same food, does your mind and heart go back to those days when your mother lovingly cared for you in your time of sickness?

Jesus knew -- and the disciples would later come to know -- just how much pain they would have each time they remembered these last few hours together. So He gave them this Last Supper to be a comfort food to them -- each and every time that they shared it, they would remember -- not just the pain, but the comfort – of his compassion.

With this precious gift from Jesus to His Disciples and to us, we are reminded each time we share – reminded of His Friendship ... with them and with us, and with all who call upon Him as the Source of Life and of Strength -- FOREVER.

Part of the Great Thanksgiving liturgy for Holy Communion also says, **"Pour out Your Holy Spirit on us gathered here, and on these gifts of bread and wine. Make them be for us the Body and Blood of Jesus Christ, that we may be for all the world the Body of Christ redeemed by His Blood."**

A Memorial Service -- yes ... and more!

Comfort Food -- yes ... and more!

Yes, much more. You see, it is the doctrine and belief of our Church that *by the Words of Jesus Himself*, This IS My Body and This IS My Blood, that when we gather around the Lord's Table for Holy Communion, the Bread and the Fruit of the Vine [the British Methodists call it "unfermented wine"] are transformed in a spiritual sense into the actual Body and Blood of Jesus Christ.

When the pastor stands before the congregation and holds the bread and cup up – the pastor stands in a line of succession from Jesus. The hands laid upon the pastor's head at ordination were from the Bishops whose heads had hands laid upon them by another, who had hands laid upon their head by another all the way back to those apostles who witnessed Jesus doing the same thing, and who received from Him the bread and wine, and were told "*This is My Body"* and "*This is My Blood*." Each ordained elder does so in Apostolic Succession -- as the Vicar (or stand in) for Christ Himself.[14]

And when each person receives, they physically feel the touch of the pastor's hand upon theirs. It's a human touch – which is so incredibly important since this is what Jesus was, and is, all about -- God with us -- Emmanuel -- God in human flesh.

---

[14] Those granted a pastoral ministry license to preach are not included within this chain of apostolic succession, as they are not ordained. This does, indeed, touch upon an area of debate within our Church. However, for the purposes of this primer on pastoral caregiving, it is sufficient to note that the Church has – for reasons of the critical importance to the Church to be able to regularly receive this blessed sacrament – licensed local pastors to celebrate and administer the Sacrament within the bounds of their local church. It is that important to the life of the Church.

How did it happen -- God in human flesh? It's a miraculous mystery. Most people call it *Virgin Birth*. But none can explain HOW it worked.

How do this bread and wine spiritually turn into the Body and Blood of Jesus? It's a mystery. None can explain it. But we believe that it is as real as Jesus said it is.

When Holy Communion is served, Jesus is once more here -- touching the recipient's hand -- their lips -- and Jesus enters into each one to feed them as miraculously as He fed the 5,000 with five loaves and two fish.

Do it too often and it is not special -- this is what I have heard. And I say, "True, but ONLY if you receive it as nothing more than a memorial service. Does praying lose its special meaning if we do it too often? Does worship lose its meaning if we do it too often? Then how can Jesus actually being here and touching us become un-special by doing it too often?

Think upon the Purpose of this Holy Meal -- it's not just to make us feel good -- although it does.

It's not just so we can get so close to Jesus as to touch Him -- although we do.

It's more -- it's to nourish us. ... for a very important task.

We -- thee and me -- have been chosen by God to be the Body of Christ in the world -- NOT just believers -- NOT just followers -- NOT just honest-do-gooders

We are the Body of Christ -- redeemed sinners -- to reconcile and heal a hurting world.

For such a task

For such a calling

We need Holy Food.

It's ordinary bread and grape juice -- but spiritually transformed into Jesus' Body and Blood.

In order that ordinary folks -- even some who have sinned a whole lot -- may be transformed into Christ's Body.

It's a mystery why God works this way -- BUT GOD DOES.

And it's a miracle. But this is what God does. Thanks be to God.

Finally, think upon that part of the Great Thanksgiving liturgy for Holy Communion which says, **"BY YOUR SPIRIT MAKE US ONE WITH CHRIST, ONE WITH EACH OTHER, AND ONE IN MINISTRY TO ALL THE WORLD, UNTIL CHRIST COMES IN FINAL VICTORY AND WE FEAST TOGETHER WITH ALL THE SAINTS AT THE HEAVENLY BANQUET. THROUGH YOUR SON JESUS CHRIST, WITH THE HOLY SPIRIT IN AND THROUGH YOUR HOLY CHURCH, ALL HONOR AND GLORY IS YOURS, ALMIGHTY GOD, NOW AND FOR EVER. AMEN."**

The first Sunday of November is the celebration of ALL SAINTS' DAY. It's one of the "feast days" (holy-days) of the Church which calls upon us to remember those who have gone on before -- and to think upon how much of who we are, is owed to them – all the saints who have gone on before, and who have made the sacrifices and contributions that made it possible for us to be here today. But their work was not completed. The 11th chapter of the Letter to the Hebrews spells out how that work is not made complete except in and through us. So that great cloud of witnesses is cheering us on – so that the work of Christ begun in them will be made complete in us. They are all at the banquet table cheering us on, and awaiting our arrival at that banquet table with them.

There's no finer image to hold onto, than the heavenly banquet we're going to eat someday.

Jesus loved to eat with folks -- so much so that He ate with sinners. Otherwise, He would have had to eat alone.

But there's going to be a another bigger dinner. And at the table are going to be Jesus, and Peter, Paul & Mary (the original ones) and St. Francis, and John & Charles Wesley, and my grandparents, too, I think -- even my grandfather that I never met -- and can you think of who else will be there – set aside this book for a moment and name them in your hearts now.

Each time we receive Holy Communion, it is an appetizer course -- we get just a foretaste, when we feed on Jesus, of that great banquet. The saints are all there now -- and sometimes when I close my eyes, I can picture them there.

And sometimes -- I can even hear them -- not just the sounds of their eating and singing and laughing -- but also their cheering -- **cheering us on**.

We heard these words: *Through Your Son, Jesus Christ, with the Holy Spirit in and through Your Holy Church. ...*

Holy Church -- that's not just us -- it's the whole great cloud of witnesses who have gone on before us. Each and every time we touch and share in Holy Food, just as the saints did while walking on earth, we are connected with them who are at the great banquet they've just begun. And when they've been there 10,000 years, they've just begun. Now that's a banquet! And in less time than that, we can join with them again, for all eternity.

The Kingdom of God -- announced by Jesus -- was and shall evermore be -- AND IS PRESENT RIGHT NOW.

God's Holy Church was and shall evermore be -- and we are invited to join right now in this Holy Appetizer course.

These are some of the reasons Holy Communion is such a wonderful and mysterious gift. It gives us the comfort and memories of Jesus' meal with His disciples -- that makes Jesus Christ my Lord present here and now -- and that celebrates a glorious *yet-to-come* -- all at the same time.

Something THAT POWERFUL begins in the local church worship setting, but it satisfies a hunger that is met in hospital bed, jail visitation room, and in shut-ins' homes. They all hunger for it.

Indeed, there is study available that shows how Alzheimer's patients, when served Holy Communion using the liturgy prevalent when they were young adults in the Church (as opposed to the present form in our Hymnal or Book of Worship) actually come out of the Alzheimer's disease that consumes them – while they are receiving the sacrament.[15]

---

[15] I highly recommend the book Elaine Ramshaw, *Ritual and Pastoral Care* (Philadelphia: Fortress Press, 1987) for discussion of this study, and for a plethora of other ways in which sacraments and liturgy of the Church have such powerful impact on pastoral caregiving.

The one common thread in *all* the scriptural accounts of Holy Communion[16] is found in the four verb action that Jesus takes with the bread.

> ➢ He <u>TAKES</u>
> ➢ <u>BLESSES</u> (give thanks)
> ➢ <u>BREAKS</u>, and
> ➢ <u>GIVES</u>

The fact that these four simple tasks are <u>always</u> used in scripture should not go unnoticed as to its significance. On the one hand, it has always been for me the very bottom line necessity of "mandatory words" that must be said in any celebration of Holy Communion.

But there is a pastoral insight from this as well. This formula:

> ➢ <u>TAKE</u>
> ➢ <u>BLESS</u> (give thanks)
> ➢ <u>BREAK</u>, and
> ➢ <u>GIVE</u>

is also a good formula for us to apply to people whose lives seemed overwhelmed by crisis, tragedy, and (particularly for pastors) overwork.

If I were to give you a twenty-five pound slab of lunch meat and tell you that you had to eat it, it might seem overwhelming. But if you were to <u>take</u> it, and <u>bless/give thanks</u> for it, <u>break</u> it into manageable bite size pieces, you would be able to <u>give</u> the task what was needed to accomplish it (with God's help) over a period of time.

I have often used that metaphor for both myself (in "crunch times") and for parishioners facing overload. It is a demonstration of how God's grace works. Surely there are times when life's situations seem to be as oppressive as the notion of trying to feed 5,000 people (plus women and children) with just a few scraps of food.

---

[16] This includes the Gospel and Pauline accounts of *The Last Supper* as well as the Gospel accounts of the miraculous feeding of the multitudes with loaves and fish (which the *Didache*, the early teaching of the Apostles, teaches is the basis for Holy Communion, rather than *The Last Supper*.

But – in bite size pieces, and fully reliant upon the miraculous *Holy Mystery* of God's working in our lives – things can be done, travail can be endured, massive responsibilities can be accomplished, and the situation can indeed be saved. There is hope!

A Nugget

"THE ISSUE" IS ALMOST NEVER
<u>THE</u> ISSUE

Remember the nugget.

How it gets played out will be as varied as people with whom you are in pastoral relationship.

The principle, generally stated, is:

> ➢ What people tell you they want to talk about
> ➢ The conflict that is going on between people
> ➢ The crisis that threatens to devastate his/her/ their life / lives
> ➢ The (to use psychologists' language) "presenting problem"

is what the person often consciously believes is the issue.

It's not.

Almost never. (I've never experienced when it *is*, but I've learned to never say "never.")

Most often he / she / they don't know that this is not the real issue, let alone what the real issue, in fact, is.

Listen carefully, prayerfully – trying to discern what <u>the</u> issue is. That means: Don't get wrapped up in trying to "fix" the issue they brought to you. If you do, you'll get sidetracked from discerning what the real issue is.

(Oh, by the way) most of the time they won't believe that "the issue" is *not* <u>the</u> issue. It rarely does much good to tell them so. Your job is to direct their attention to clues or signs that allows them to "discover" what <u>the</u> real issue is, and to "discover" that it really is <u>the</u> real issue.

The good news: by prayerfully, carefully pointing to those clues or signs, the pastoral care receiver may discover <u>the</u> issue before you do. That's OK, too. Remember: it's not about you.

9
Wishing and Hoping

When you wish upon a star,
makes no difference who you are
Anything your heart desires
will come to you.
If your heart is in your dreams,
no request is too extreme
When you wish upon a star
as dreamers do.

Ah, do you remember the song Jiminy Cricket sang to Pinocchio? This – down deep in the hearts of many of our parishioners – is what God is about. God is the Big One in the Sky Who, if we pray right and live right, will grant our wishes.

This, they can handle, pretty much on their own. But when, in the dirtiness and messiness of life, God does *not* respond like Jiminy Cricket, then the pastor is sometimes called upon (a) to make the prayers in the proper way, using her or his good connections, to make sure the wish comes true; or (b) to explain what went wrong. Why does God, if God really is good, treat me like this?

Whether the request is for (a) or (b), the answer to (b) is what you need to work on.

It is a problem as old as Adam and Eve banished from the Garden of Eden. It is the reason why the Book of Job has resonated over the centuries with so many people. The answers are not pat, nor simple. It is the *theodicy* problem (either God is all good and not all powerful, or God is all powerful and not so good.)

Henri J. M. Nouwen captured a significant distinction when he said that "WISHING" is different from "HOPING." We Christians are a people of Hope; Jiminy Cricket and the dreamers are creatures of wishfulness.

Wishing is making a list, checking it twice, allowing God to find out who's been naughty and nice, and then giving all the "wishes" to those who have been nice.

Hoping is believing that the God of Resurrection is still at work in God's creation, and that God's Will shall be accomplished. Resurrection, if only a once-in-history event, is surely still a wonderful thing. But, if Jesus is *the pioneer and perfecter of our faith* (Hebrews 12:2) then His Resurrection was just the first, and God still Resurrects all around us. It is where God still takes dead ends and turns them into new beginnings.

Hope is different from Wishing, in that Hope is open-ended. Wishing is only satisfied when God does "it" the way we want it.

> [1]Therefore, since we are justified by faith, we have peace with God through our Lord Jesus Christ, [2]through whom we have obtained access to this grace in which we stand; and we boast in our hope of sharing the glory of God. [3]And not only that, but we also boast in our sufferings, knowing that suffering produces endurance, [4]and endurance produces character, and character produces hope, [5]and *hope does not disappoint us*, because God's love has been poured into our hearts through the Holy Spirit that has been given to us. (Romans 5)

Wishing will often disappoint us. Hope does not.

But, it is an incredibly difficult thing to *walk by faith, not by sight* when the manure is falling down on us. It is, admittedly, much easier to see it all when we look into the rear view mirror (which, indeed, may be what *faith* is – knowing that someday we *will* be able to look into the rear view mirror and see how Hope was vindicated.)

Part of the problem with Wishing is that we don't have enough knowledge, or a long enough vision, to know what to wish for. If you don't believe me – follow me through just one little test. Remember the story of Joseph and his jealous brothers (Genesis 36-50)

➢ When Joseph is seventeen, Jacob, his father, gives him a beautiful, expensive robe. [*That's* good.]

➢ No, that's bad. It makes his 10 older brothers insanely jealous of Joseph, and they plot to murder him [*That's* bad.]

➢ No, that's good, because they decide to sell him into slavery rather than kill him, and Joseph ends up in the house of Egyptian official Potiphar, who likes Joseph so much, he puts Joseph in charge of managing his entire household. [*That's* good.]

➢ No, that's bad. You see, Potiphar's wife is physically attracted to Joseph and she tries to seduce him. [*That's* bad.]

➢ You're right, that *is* bad...*but* Joseph refuses to let her have her way with him. [*That's* good.]

➢ Well, you're right, that *is* good...*except* she won't take "no" for an answer, and one day, when there is no one around, *she* pulls his robe off him, and *he* runs out of the house. [*That's* good.]

➢ No, that's bad. Even though nothing happened, she accuses him of trying to rape her. [Oooh, *that's* bad.]

➢ No, that's good. He never has to worry about her again. [*That's* good.]

➢ No, that's bad. He's thrown into prison for years! [*That's* bad.]

➢ No, that's good. Once again, God blesses Joseph so much that he becomes the jailer's personal assistant. Then when Pharaoh needs some dreams interpreted the jailer refers Joseph, who does such a good job interpreting the dreams that Pharaoh makes Joseph second-in-command of all Egypt. And when Joseph uses his God-given wisdom, he saves enough grain during bumper crop years that they have plenty during seven years of famine to save all the people of Egypt and those from Israel – including Joseph's whole family. And when Joseph's family comes to Egypt they have a big happy reunion, with all previous wrongs forgiven. [*That's* good.]

➢ No, that's bad. Because, after all of the Israelites move to Egypt, the Pharaoh friend of Joseph dies and the new Pharaoh has a different immigration policy, and he puts all the Israelites into slavery. [*That's* bad]

➢ Well, it might seem bad, but that situation gave God the opportunity to perform the most incredible act in human history to date – since the flood in Noah's day – and the Israelites are freed, through the parting of the Sea; and they return to the Promised Land, reshaped into a nation of God's Chosen People, instead of just a wandering tribe. And they still celebrate every year that Deliverance of God. [*That's* good]

Good? Bad? Sometimes it's really hard trying to make up our minds.

So often, we have that problem: we don't know enough of what is involved – both now and how it's going to work out down the road – we don't know enough to <u>wish</u> for the right thing. And then we get disappointed whenever it doesn't turn out how we had wished.

But instead of wishing upon a star, we can place our Hope in God, who does not disappoint.

Do you know the poem "Tapestry"?

> My life is but a tapestry
> Between my Lord and me.
> I cannot choose the colors;
> He worketh steadily.
>
> Oftimes He weaveth sorrow,
> And I in foolish pride
> Forget He sees the upper
> And I, the underside.

Not 'til the loom is silent
And the shuttles cease to fly
Shall God unroll the canvas
And explain the reason why.

> The dark threads are as needful
> In the Weaver's skilful hand
> As the threads of gold and silver
> In the pattern He has planned.

Corrie ten Boom was a very young woman incarcerated with her sister in a Nazi concentration camp. Just before her sister died in that concentration camp, she told Corrie: "Tell people what we have learned here … that there is no pit so deep that God is not deeper still. They will listen, because we have been here." I don't know if Corrie ten Boom also knew the "Tapestry" poem you just read, but for the next forty years of her life, she did what her sister told her. She told people: "*Although the threads of my life have often seemed knotted, I know, by faith, that on the other side of the embroidery there is a crown.*"

The hard reality of life is:

1. We all get manure dumped in our lives. It always seems at the time that it is more than others have. And the reality is that we can always find some people who have more than we do. It just never seems that way at the moment.

2. Nothing in the Bible ever tells us that we have a right to "no manure." Although our question is so often "WHY ME?" there is nothing in the Bible that would contradict the question "WHY NOT YOU?"

3. Manure can help us grow. Remember Jesus' story of the gardener in Luke 13:

   [6]Then he told this parable: "A man had a fig tree planted in his vineyard; and he came looking for fruit on it and found none. [7]So he said to the gardener, 'See here! For three years I have come looking for fruit on this fig tree, and still I find none. Cut it down! Why should it be wasting the soil?' [8]He replied, 'Sir, *let it alone for one more year, until I dig around it and put manure on*

105

> *it.* ⁹If it bears fruit next year, well and good; but if not, you can cut it down.'"

Manure works in our life, when we allow God to work in our lives. And God tends to work through Resurrection Power. We can't figure it out in advance. The religious leaders of Jerusalem, in 29 A.D., thought they had all the bases covered. Everyone thought that the "Jesus situation" had come to a dead end. After all, crucifixion did have a painfully final nature to it. And then, God, like some incredible jokester, popped up like a jack-in-the-box and said: SURPRISE!

And that's how God still works today. We may be able to figure it out, looking backwards, but it's daggone tough to figure out how God is going to work ahead of time.

Manure stinks!! And there are lots of things in life that stink. I don't say that God puts these stinky things on us. But I do know that God's power is at work in even the deepest pile of manure – if we allow.

We always have different options with manure. Some people like the **WALLOW IN IT** option. *"Woe is me. Woe is me. Woe is me. Woe is me. ...."* (best understood when read in your best Eeyore Donkey voice) Like Garrison Keillor says, *"The trouble with feeling sorry for yourself is that it feels so good, that it's hard to quit it."*

A second option is **TO FLING IT**. (Translation: you become a fan that the manure hits.) These people just strike out at others. Anger is often a natural first response. And that's OK. But, if we get stuck in that response, it becomes just like wallowing. It doesn't help and it drives away those who love us and it certainly never bears fruit.

A third option is **TO WATCH IT UNFOLD**. Anne Lamott was gifted by a spiritual friend during one of the dark times of her soul. She learned that manure gets piled up around us, sometimes, to distract us from a wonderful thing that God is in the process of birthing. We are distracted by the manure so we won't come over and "help" God, *i.e.* interfere with the wonderful thing God is doing, until it is ready for us to receive.

I read once about a fat man who really worked very hard to lose weight. He did very well, particularly with a special temptation – driving past a bakery each morning on the way to his job. One morning, the temptation was "almost" more than he could bear. So he "made a deal with God." He said that he would drive right by the bakery and not get a big sugar glazed cinnamon roll, if that's what God wanted. But, if God really wanted him to stop and have this one "little treat," then God would open up a parking place right in front of the bakery. And, sure enough – after he had driven around the block thirteen times -- there was a parking place right in front!

We sometimes "find" God working in some pretty bizarre ways in our lives – fulfilling our "wishes." And yet, too often we are not patient enough to allow God's work to unfold in the midst of the manure.

So we each get to choose what to with the manure in our life?

- Wallow in it
- Fling it
- Watch a new birth

Joan Chittester put it like this:

GOD IS LIFE, NOT A VENDING MACHINE FULL OF TRIFLES TO FIT THE WHIMS OF THE HUMAN RACE.

THE CONTEMPLATIVE PRAYS IN ORDER TO BE OPEN TO WHAT IS, RATHER THAN TO RESHAPE THE WORLD TO THEIR OWN LESSER DESIGNS.

As pastoral caregivers, we need to be contemplatives, so as to help people learn to HOPE AND WAIT, instead of WISH AND WALLOW OR FLING.

DON'T BE SURPRISED IF SOMEONE YOU HAVE BEEN COUNSELING FOR A PERIOD OF TIME SUDDENLY STOPS COMING TO WORSHIP

During pastoral counseling sessions, the parishioner may be comfortable enough to finally open up – revealing to you (and perhaps to themself for the first time) their deep feelings – warts and all. You are making progress.

You surely have had, and will have, people after a sermon say to you, "Preacher, I felt like you were talking to just me today in the sermon." It usually is meant as a compliment that your sermon was particularly relevant to their life.

However, to someone who has bared their soul before you in counseling, that sort of comment – Preacher, I felt like you were talking to just me in the sermon – is a very real feeling. They feel like they have personally been laid out naked / vulnerable before the whole church.

It has nothing to do with your actually doing so. It just feels like that to them.

There's not really much you can do about it.

I have sometimes wondered if it might help, at the beginning of a counseling relationship, to explain that possibility, and how you will never violate the confidentiality of these times together – even in anonymity; that these times together are not the fodder for your sermon.

It might work. But that involves the head having control over the emotions. And that rarely happens.

Sometimes really good pastoral caregiving causes you to lose a member. But if it's good pastoral caregiving, you have helped another church receive a good, healthy, member. And that's not bad. It's not about you.

10
Keep Your Sword Sharp

^{15b}Always be ready to make your defense to anyone who demands from you an accounting for the hope that is in you; ¹⁶yet do it with gentleness and reverence. Keep your conscience clear, so that, when you are maligned, those who abuse you for your good conduct in Christ may be put to shame. (1 Peter 3)

¹²Indeed, the word of God is living and active, sharper than any two-edged sword, piercing until it divides soul from spirit, joints from marrow; it is able to judge the thoughts and intentions of the heart. (Hebrews 4)

The Word of God is indeed a two edged sword. Sometimes it is wielded in such a way as to "cut through" the arguments and contentions of "an opponent." Indeed, Satan was a skilled adversary in the application of scriptural swordsmanship with Jesus in the wilderness.

111

In pastoral caregiving, scripture is not used to "prove a point" or to "cut down an opponent." In pastoral caregiving, the pastor is walking alongside the parishioner, helping her or him discover that which will help them open up, see more deeply, and put back together the pieces of life that are difficult to hold together, so as to make that life meaningful and (as Jesus said He intended it) abundant – even in the midst of pain.

Sometimes, scriptures are used in the Church like "bumper stickers."

> [2c] we boast in our hope of sharing the glory of God. [3]And not only that, but we also boast in our sufferings, knowing that suffering produces endurance, [4]and endurance produces character, and character produces hope, [5]and hope does not disappoint us, because God's love has been poured into our hearts through the Holy Spirit that has been given to us. (Romans 5)

> [28]We know that all things work together for good for those who love God, who are called according to his purpose. (Romans 8)

Bumper sticker platitudes are "nice" and they are easily mumbled, for lack of something else to say, at the funeral home. And, for folks who have never heard them, they may be of some value. But, usually, at the time of the intervention of the pastoral caregiver in time of personal crisis, these platitudes don't really help uncover, understand with the heart, and put back together. Following that process, scriptures used in such a way may indeed be beneficial "reminders" of the journey taken (much in the same way bumper stickers from vacation spots are used.)

The Word of God is truly a powerful tool – a two edged sword. And it is indeed the place where God's people can go to find help in times of trouble. (The Psalms are a particularly good place to go, when joining in the prayers of God's people during times of angst and lament.) But the scriptures are not so much an "answer" as they are a "tool" for hurting or searching people to use in the hard and difficult job of working out our salvation "with fear and trembling."

It should be noted, as well, that the word "salvation," as used in the News Testament, is often a translation of the

Greek word *sozo*. *Sozo* certainly means more than "getting to heaven" salvation, in much the same way that the Hebrew word *shalom* means more than "peace." *Sozo* also means "healing" and "wholeness." Working our way into that is indeed struggle, which requires both human and divine effort (grace.) Thomas Merton suggested that St. Paul's admonition to *work out or salvation with fear and trembling* is an accurate description for the hard work of soul healing, which involves stripping away the masks that we have been putting on, one over the other, for most of our lives.

God's Word in scripture is particularly helpful in this process when we use the "story" component of scripture.

In a playful midrash, it is said that when God was looking about creation for a "chosen people," the Romans were first approached. They pledged that if God chose them, they would provide a strong, safe, peaceful kingdom, with a good infrastructure, to promote the Kingdom of God on earth. God also asked the Greeks what they would offer. They said that they had the ability to apply an elaborate system of philosophical thought, beautiful temples, and divine hierarchy to the implementation of God's Reign upon the earth. God thanked them for the offer, and moved down the road to ask the Jews what they would offer. Being shrewd bargainers, the Jews said that if they were the chosen people of God, they could offer a wonderful storytelling legacy for the establishment of God's Kingdom. And God, also a shrewd bargainer, accepted.

Although that is "playful," there is also a strong element of truth in it. So much of the time, we think of (and act out) our religion as a system of rules and structures meant to give meaning and direction to life. Yet, when we look at the Bible, we see that the "first [written] commandment" recorded doesn't come until after 69 chapters of story -- all 50 chapters of Genesis and the first 19 chapters of Exodus.

One of the reasons Jesus' messiahship was not recognized by the religious leaders was that whenever they questioned Him, they expected a messiah to answer with a rule or commandment. Instead, so often when He was asked a question, His response was, "Let me tell you a story ...."

113

Story has power. It allows the reader / hearer to enter in – to enter into the story as a way of entering into relationship with God.

Jalaluddin Rumi, a poet of the 13th century, spoke of a poem entitled *Story-Water*. He compares a story to bath water. The bath water is heated by fire. The heated water now carries messages from the fire to the body. It lets the flame and the skin meet. Rumi notes:

Very few can sit down
In the middle of the fire itself …
We need intermediaries

Stories are intermediaries between "the fire itself" (God's Spirit) and those who would be warmed by it.[17]

The good pastoral caregiver knows her/his Bible well enough to be able to refer the quester to a good story, where they can be touched by the warmth of the Spirit. The story doesn't tell them what to do; it invites them into relationship with God, where they can discover the course they need to take.

A seminary colleague told the story of how he ended up in seminary. He was a gifted musician and was pursuing that study in college. But he felt a constant gnawing on the inside. Something wasn't right. He could find no peace. He didn't know if perhaps he was being called into pastoral ministry – or what? So, one day, he decided to go talk to the chaplain at his college. He laid out the whole scenario of what he had been going through. She listened carefully and thoughtfully. Then she said simply, "Go read the 19th chapter of 1 Kings. If you want to talk some more, then come back."

Period.

My friend was a bit miffed. Like Naaman the Syrian visiting Elisha (2 Kings 5:1-12) he had expected "a bit more." But, he followed her advice and read the story of Elijah in flight from Jezebel, and read it again, and again. Each time, his mind kept tripping over one expression: "What are you doing here, Elijah?" – except that he heard it in his mind

---

[17] John Shea, *Gospel Light, Jesus Stories for Spiritual Consciousness* (New York: Crossroad, 1999), p. 9.

as, "What are you doing here, Philip?" He thus wrestled for quite some time.

Then he returned to the chaplain to talk to her about what he needed to do to enter seminary, to fulfill the answer with which he had come to peace. Philip told me that each Sunday morning, when he climbs into the pulpit, he is greeted by a sign affixed to the pulpit that reads: "What are you doing here?" It is his reminder, both of the story of his call, and of the purpose of that call: he is not there to share "his thoughts." He is there to be a spokesperson for the very Lord God Almighty.

Good pastoral caregivers are able to listen carefully and thoughtfully, and to discern a Word from the Lord as to the right story to apply. That takes a deep knowledge of the Bible, which is always in need of refreshing. It means "keeping your sword sharp."

The Bible is full of wonderful stories that apply to the complexities of contemporary life, and are good fuel for the pastoral care setting.

For his whole life, Jacob had been a control freak – always wanted to be in charge, to dictate the terms. Then he came to a wrestling match on the edge of the River Jabbok. Even, as the wrestling match was drawing to a close, at the break of day, <u>Jacob was trying to dicker with God</u>. And the story tells us how that worked out. (Genesis 32:22-31)

Jacob demanded a blessing. (He was fond of those; that's how he got into trouble with Esau to begin with.) Instead, he got a name: no longer would his name be Jacob, but Israel.

So then Jacob demanded a name – his opponent's name. And instead, God gave him a blessing. If you're a control freak, that's just go to drive you crazy!!

Perhaps, just perhaps, Jacob was getting the idea. Just to make sure, <u>God wounded his hip, so Jacob would have to spend the rest of his life, leaning on God for support.</u>

That's what happens sometimes – we think life is not going well. And we try to get control of it. But it's in the messiness of life's pains and problems that we have to let go and let God, and it's here where we find THE WAY.

Life is messy. And so are the stories from the Bible.

➢ Just as the Bible's human story begins with a man and a woman sinning in a garden;

➢ just as God's choice of nations begins with a beautiful woman and her weak husband, who offered her body to other men to save his own skin;

➢ just as the saving of that nation from slavery begins with a reluctant murderer at a burning bush;

➢ just as the entry into the land of promise begins with two spies and a prostitute;

➢ just as the beginning of the kingship of that nation begins with an insensitive husband, a foolish priest, an arrogant co-wife, and a barren woman who dares to make demands from God for dignity and respect;

➢ just as the greatest kingship of that country would involve lust and murder, adultery and betrayal;

➢ and just as the Christian story begins with a humiliated man and his much-too-young pregnant girlfriend –

so very often the grand episodes of a powerful God at work are found in very domestic and earthy moments. And God never seems to shy away from times when we've *gone down to the threshing floor.*[18]

We all remember the story of Jesus and the woman caught in adultery, from John chapter 8. She was confronted by the religious leaders, clearly guilty as charged. But Jesus didn't seem to want to punish her. Indeed, careful review of the story indicates that Jesus did not wait until she asked for forgiveness (she is never recorded as having done so) but just gave it to her. And then, if we pay careful attention, we see Jesus' format for how forgiveness works: first comes forgiveness, and *then* comes repentance afterwards. He simply and powerfully placed a crown of glory over that woman's head, a crown which she spent the rest of her life claiming and living so as to grow into it.

One of my favorite authors, in the field of story and spirituality, John Shea, has a favorite task for small groups

---

[18] The "threshing floor" reference is to the thinly disguised scatological manner in which Ruth seduced Boaz (Ruth 3:1-11) The thin disguise is revealed by good scriptural scholarship, which reveals that when the word "feet" is used in the story, it is a euphemism for the male sex organ.

(although it also works in one on one settings.) He likes to ask people to tell him their favorite, or most important, story from the Bible. They are not allowed to actually look at the text – just tell the story. Then he will ask them what the story means to them.

One time he did this, a young man told him his version of that John 8 story of the woman caught in the act of adultery and brought before Jesus. After he told his version of the story, he said that it was the most important story for him, because everyone is holding a rock.

"What do you mean?" asked Shea.

"Everyone wants to stone someone. We go through every day of our lives holding these stones. There's a stone for each person who has done us wrong.

"In the Bible story, Jesus didn't let them throw their stones at this woman; they all just walked away carrying their stones with them.

"We all do it. Everyone around me is carrying stones. I figure some of them have my name on them.

"As for me, I'm so tired of carrying all these stones. Jesus won't let me use them to stone anyone, so I just keep on carrying them. I just wish I could get rid of them, because they are weighing me down. Nobody gets stoned; we all just get worn down.

"I wish I could lay down my stones. But I just can't do it. I just can't do it."

Shea was tempted to tell the young man that this is not what the John 8 story was about – about people carrying their stones. He wanted to tell him about all of the exegetical reasons why the young man had misread the story.

But he didn't – because he realized that this young man had allowed God's Spirit to work through this particular story in a way that others had not seen. And, so interpreted, this story had exposed a wound in his soul, for which he was hungering for God's help in healing.

This is a tremendous tool for the pastoral counselor, so long as her/his sword is sharp enough to be able to pick out where the storyteller speaking strays from the text that is in the Bible. In that variation, the skillful pastor will often discern what is at the heart of the parishioner's heartache.

Know your scriptures; know them well. And be open to God's direction for how the divine-human story that has been written and passed down through the millennia can be applied to the divine-human story that is being lived in your presence.

THE THREE MOST IMPORTANT

RULES FOR PASTORAL CAREGIVING

AND

FOR EFFECTIVE MINISTRY:

(YOU MAY HAVE HAPPENED TO HAVE READ THESE BEFORE, BUT THEY DESERVE TO BE REPEATED.)

➢ LEARN THEM,

➢ MEMORIZE THEM,

➢ WEAR THEM ON YOUR HEART AND BEFORE YOUR EYES, AND (CERTAINLY) AS A BRAKE ON YOUR TONGUE.

1. LOVE YOUR PEOPLE.

2. LOVE YOUR PEOPLE.

3. LOVE YOUR PEOPLE.

11
ABBA, GIVE ME A WORD

Once upon a time, a parachutist got caught in a terrific gale, which blew him fifty miles off course. He landed, with his chute caught in the limbs of a tree. He hung there for hours, until a man came along. The parachutist hollered out, "Hey! Can you tell me where I am."

And the one who was walking along said, "You're in a tree."

And the parachutist said, "Oh, you must be a preacher."

And, somewhat surprised, the preacher who happened along, said, "How did you know that?"

And the parachutist said, "Because you told me something that is certainly true, and, just as certainly, completely useless."

"The essence of the spirituality of the desert is that it was not taught but caught; it was a whole way of life. It was not an esoteric doctrine or a predetermined plan of ascetic practice that would be learned and applied. The father, or

121

'abba', was not the equivalent of the Zen Buddhist 'Master'. It is important to understand this, because there really is no way of talking about *the* way of prayer, or *the* spiritual teaching of the desert fathers. They did not have a systematic *way*; they had the hard work and experience of a lifetime of striving to re-direct every aspect of body, mind, and soul to God, and that is what they talked about. That, also, is what they meant by prayer: prayer was not an activity undertaken for a few hours each day; it was a life continually turned toward God."[19]

It was the practice of the monks in the desert to come to the Abba, and ask: "Abba, give me a word." The response by the "wise old man" (as they were often affectionately called) would be a short and simple instruction or expression. The monk would then take "the word" and "chew" on it, sometimes for days, weeks, and (sometimes documented, even) years.

Some of the "words" that have been recorded for posterity include these:

➢ An old man said, "Do not agree with every word. Be slow to believe, quick to speak the truth."

➢ Abba Sarmatas said: I prefer a sinful man who knows he has sinned and repents, to a man who has not sinned and considers himself to be righteous.

➢ An old man said, "Even though the saints suffer here below, yet have they in part already received rest." He said this because they were set free from all worldly cares.

➢ Abba Zeno said, 'If a man wants God to hear his prayer quickly, then before he prays for anything else, even his own soul, when he stands and stretches out his hands towards God, he must pray with all his heart for his enemies. Through this action God will hear everything that he asks.'

---

[19] Sister Benedicta Ward, SLG, transl., The Wisdom of the Desert Fathers [Apophthegmata Patrum (The Anonymous Series)], Fairacres, Oxford: SLG Press, 1975) p. xii

➢ An old man said, "Do not be intimate with the abbot and do not visit him much, for you will learn a certain over-familiarity of speech from it and finally you will want to be superior in your turn.

➢ Amma Syncletica said: It is possible to be a solitary in one's mind while living in a crowd, and it is possible for one who is a solitary to live in the crowd of his own thoughts.

There is real power in "giving a word."

It's harder to dodge "a word" than it is to dodge a whole sermon.

It's harder to forget "a word" than it is to forget a whole sermon.

It's easier to "chew" on "a word" than to chew on a whole sermon.

The reality is that, particularly in pastoral caregiving situations, people will so often hear *just* "a word." Regardless of how much is spoken, it will be *just* "a word" that lingers.

I am still amazed when a member of the flock says to me something like, "I still think about what you said to me two years ago, when you said ...." It happens more frequently that I would ever imagine.

If they are going to hear *just* "a word," how much better it is when it is "a word" carefully and prayerfully chosen, instead of just a chance phrase in the midst of a whole monologue.

The pastor must be neatly in tune with THE Word – creative, discerning, powerful God-Word – in order to "give a word" that is right and proper for the specific pastoral care situation. Such is anything but an easy task, which might explain, in part, why "Abba, give me a word" is not practiced very much, today.

When the pastor "receives" "a word" to give, with the assurance that it is "the Word of the Lord," then s/he needs to give it in faith.

➢ Offer it to the parishioner
➢ Just let it sit there
➢ Let the parishioner chew on it (or ignore it, if they so choose)

> ➢ And then neither retract nor defend it
> ➢ Even if the parishioner initially really disagrees with the "word" you have given
> ➢ But let them discuss it, if they choose

I remember a time when my CPE supervisor gave me "a word" with which I strongly disagreed. He was not threatened by my protestations of its non-applicability. Instead, he merely asked me to tell him about it.

A pastoral caregiver who "needs to be right" will make a terrible mistake if s/he argues with the parishioner – trying to "prove" their wisdom.

My CPE supervisor – who clearly evidenced a nonchalance about needing my approval in order to maintain his own self-worth – simply asked me to tell him how or why he was wrong.

Then he responded (again seemingly nonchalantly, but now I recognize how much thought, prayer, and hard work went into his responses) with questions that did not threaten me, nor attempt to justify himself. But his responses caused me to dig deeper into "that word" which he had spoken – both in that moment and many times later (sometimes, even still today.)

I clearly remembered leaving our session with the very clear conclusion that he really didn't know me at all. Nonetheless, I was still haunted by the very clear memory of the singularity of "that word."

I didn't have a whole sermon nor monologue – a lot of ideas to think about. There was just that one nagging "word," that one pink elephant that I couldn't seem to forget. It kept popping up again and again in both my thinking and in my praying.

There were indeed some "word"s given over the course of our several meetings these many years ago that still come to my mind. Some of them I am still convinced that he was wrong. But that doesn't matter, for as I have danced through the years with such "word"s, even if I have not become persuaded by their accuracy, I have been nonetheless blessed by the dance.

If his goal had been to "be right," then in some of these instances, he failed. But, if his goal had been to plant a seed that would not be forgotten and which would compel me to have several long dances with Jesus, during which my life in Christ would be enlivened, then my he did a slam-bang good job.

I've figured out by now that the latter goal was surely what he was about. And I've sought him out on different occasions and thanked him for having done this. He's been polite, and appropriately responsive to my remarks of appreciation. But that which enabled him to "give me a word" was his recognition of his worth as being from God Who made him, and was not dependent upon my approval.

That inward assurance gives the pastoral caregiver the ability

➢ and power or discernment to <u>receive</u> "a word" from God,

➢ to <u>give</u> "a word" to someone who asks for it,

➢ and to <u>trust</u> (even without any present expression from the parishioner) that this word "will not fall to the ground." (1 Samuel 3:19)

A Nugget

DON'T TAKE NOTES

This may come easy for some and difficult for others. That depends on basic personality and on prior habits.

As a trial attorney, it came difficult for me. I wanted to make sure I got all of the details. I didn't trust my memory.

I was finally given to understand: it's more important to be totally present with the person – and for them to know that I am totally present – than it is to get all of the details.

Guess what? My memory got better.

And even more importantly – I got more details.

You can't understand what a person is saying to you unless you are able to look deep into their eyes, to be unoccupied by note taking so as to be able to carefully and prayerfully pay attention to "the whole package" of the person before you.

The one exception may be when it comes to planning a funeral, and you are gathering a lot of information about the one who has gone on to be with Jesus. I usually divide that time into two segments (1) where I am paying careful, prayerful attention to the family members to whom I am talking; (2) where I am taking copious notes about their remembrances of their departed loved one. But, even here, it is important to not let (2) overtake (1), because the purpose of (2) is to enable you to do a better job at (1) during the funeral.

Don't ever forget the purpose, by being so caught up in the details. You are a Doctor of Souls, a Vicar of Christ.

127

12
Funerals

O God, ... speak to us once more your solemn message of life and of death. Help us to live as those who are prepared to die.
The United Methodist Book of Worship, page 142

Jacqueline Kennedy Onassis was once reported to have said, "The Church is at its best, at time of funerals." The reporter of this quotation found this interesting, since the former first lady's opinion of the Church was reputed to be pretty low.

I found two truths in that reported quotation: (1) The Church *should indeed* be at her best at the time of funerals. There is no time in human living where emotions are more profound, devastation is closer to the surface, and there is a greater need to be embraced by a loving God and Body of Christ, on earth – the Church. (2) There is rarely a time in which people, even those who have felt dis-engaged from the Church for however long, are more likely to be open to the Church.

In my ministry, there is a cardinal rule: FUNERALS TRUMP.

There is nothing in ministry that takes a higher priority than in providing the solace needed at this time.

A corollary to that is: nothing takes more of my time as a pastor than in providing good pastoral care attendant to death.

Perhaps the corollary to that is: [since it takes more of my time than anything else] nothing is done with greater skill and attention, in short: nothing is done better than the funeral ministry.

People need it. The Church should provide it.

I am a bit hesitant to say the following, because I would not want anyone to infer that this is the reason for these rules and corollaries: I have had no greater success in leading people to a salvific relationship with God through Jesus Christ, and/or bringing them back into the life of the Church, than as a result of funeral ministry. That's the result – from a combination of intense need and intentionally excellent efforts to meet that need. But, that is not the reason to do it. You do it, *because it's the right thing to do*.

In death and funeral ministry, I want to make contact with the family as soon as possible – but within their comfort level. (That "within" proviso carries much weight in this area of ministry, because *provision of comfort to troubled souls* is the primary motivation.)

For some people, this can be a completely new experience. The more guidance the pastor can give in telling folks what is going to happen, the better they will be.

You need to recognize (and I frequently tell close relatives to not be surprised if/when they experience this) that loved ones in the grief process will often have what feels like a *fugue state / dissociative reaction*. In other words, they will feel like they are outside the events looking in, seeing themselves going through motions, but not feeling like they are really *in* the situation. I tell them that this is a normal grief defense mechanism, and that it doesn't mean they are going crazy.

As part of my pre-funeral ritual, I offer (and encourage) to meet with the family at the funeral home. Sometimes I can be helpful to them in planning things, or in helping them understand how parts of this massively confusing puzzle fit together. It also gives me an opportunity to get a first glimpse at what the funeral worship will look like (and be on the same page with the funeral director.)[20]

In discussing the arrangements with the family (at the funeral home and/or at the family's home later) I try to find out what scriptures and hymns were meaningful to the departed one (and to them – they are the ones who will be listening for a word of comfort.) I have, on occasion (when they can't think of any such scriptures) asked if the departed loved one had a personal Bible that I might peruse. I have sometimes found margin notes that have not only "tagged" the scriptures I will use, but have become the gist of the direction the funeral homily takes.

There are two options that I always offer the family. I try my best not to express any preference. My job is to provide a worship of comfort and consolation; what works for them is not necessarily what would work for me.

(1)   The celebration of Holy Communion at the funeral. This is often a new concept for families. The United Methodist Book of Worship includes Holy Communion as part of the liturgy in the Celebration of Death and Resurrection. I explain to the

---

[20]   A motivation for my doing this, early in my pastoral ministry, was also the *protection* of the family. Although I am very happy to report that such instances of need are extraordinarily rare, there have been occasions where my presence as a pastor has prevented (what shall I say) "enthusiastically sales oriented" funeral directors from taking advantage of the family – providing services that they neither need nor want. I did learn early on that it is also a good idea to make sure that a close member of the family (and yet not so close as to be so emotionally involved; *i.e.* has clearer judgment) goes with the family member to sign the interment paperwork at the cemetery. Cemeteries (which are *not* under the same governmental regulation as funeral homes) can and have seriously taken advantage of people in that moment of paper signing. Once (the occasion for my learning this lesson) I did have to "switch hats" from pastor to lawyer in following up with a cemetery which had somehow convinced a distraught husband that the prepaid everything would really be much better if an extra $3,000 were spent on a super deluxe titanium something-or-other with the vault. I played the "lawyer card" after hearing from another family member of what had happened, and all was restored to the original prepaid, agreed upon arrangements.

family (similar to the explanation in chapter 8) how the family and friends at the funeral will be sharing in the appetizer course of the banquet which their loved one is now celebrating. They get to share a meal together at the funeral.

The response to this suggestion I have found to vary quite a bit from geographic area to area. In some areas, I've had about 40% of my funerals include Holy Communion. In my present appointment, it's about 75%. In *all* instances where we have included Holy Communion, the family has thanked me, afterwards, saying that it added significantly to the worship experience of the funeral, and helped them.

(2) The "Naming" component to a funeral. I'm not sure why it bears that name; it's understood in the vernacular as "open mike time." This is a time when the pastor invites any who wish, to come forward to say "a few words" of remembrance about the departed one. Three things can happen with a "naming." Two of them are not good. (a) An appropriate number of people can come forward and speak an appropriate amount of time, and closure is assisted. (This one is the rarest occurrence.) (b) People get really cranked up and go on and on and on … The family gets worn out, and they wonder why they ever asked that this be done. (c) The grief is too close to the edge, and no one wants to come forward. The pastor says something along the lines of, "I know that all of us have many memories that could be shared, but sometimes it's just too hard to give them voice at this time." And, in the meanwhile, the family is thinking thoughts like: (i) why didn't <u>I</u> get up and speak; oh, I'm a lousy daughter/son/etc. <u>or</u> (ii) why didn't that so-and-so get up and speak; s/he's the one who has the gift of gab <u>or</u> (iii) Geez, I guess nobody liked my beloved after all; where are all his/her friends when I need them?

Like I said, three things are possible; two of them are bad; and (in my experience) the good one occurs pretty infrequently.

I try to always make some arrangement to meet with the family to share their memories (even if I have met with them at the funeral home.) I freely allow them to think that this is something I need to help me prepare the funeral. And, often – particularly if I didn't know the deceased well – it does. But, even if I knew the person like my own family member, I still always try to do this. It's an important therapeutic time for them to be able to give voice to memories, even frustrations, in a safe environment -- usually in their home. Although I will do it in my office if the family prefers; some people are just chronically (and needlessly) embarrassed by their own housekeeping, or have other reasons why they're more comfortable to meet in my office.

This gathering together also gives me an opportunity to get more details about what the family would find comforting as part of the worship. Sometimes they will provide answers to questions I asked at the funeral home, which they didn't know how to answer while they were there. It's also a time in which I can "size up" some family dynamics. Sometimes funeral settings, with the intensity of emotions already in place, can turn into mini-war zones between families that had "issues" prior to this. Being aware of this from an in-home meeting makes it easier to be pastoral at the funeral.

When I am with the family here, I try once more, to explain what is going to happen; what they can expect – even if I did so at the funeral home -- because not everything "registers" well during this season in life. I try to explain (and I follow this up often in my after-funeral care of the family) that the grief process takes a minimum of 2-3 years to work through. We have a tendency in American culture today to do everything on a fast track. Culture may have changed to a faster pace, but that does not mean that the grief process has. I warn them that they should not expect to "be over" this in any less time than 2-3 years.

I also explain to them that they *must* go through the grief process; you can't go under it, or over it, or around it. If they choose to try to not go *through* it, they will just elongate the time that it takes to process. It doesn't matter how much you might fool even your conscious thought that you are OK just right away. You can "shove it down" all you want; it will not go away, and it will find a way to break out.

It's not fun, I tell them. It will hurt – and hurt a lot. And the hole left by the loss will never completely go away, nor be filled. But, eventually the jagged edges of that hole in their life will become less painful and jagged. Love works that way.

When it comes time to prepare the funeral, I use pretty standard language that our Book of Worship provides. There is some comfort in hearing the sameness of good liturgy in these moments (like Psalm 23 – and *that* must be in the King James Version!) But the homily itself is always very individualized. We are celebrating both the Victory Jesus offers <u>and</u> the wonder and glory of the life that was lived by this beloved child of God, who was precious and beautiful to behold.

I have to confess that I can hardly bear to sit through a funeral where the preacher's message is

(a) obviously off the cuff, evidencing little to no preparation;

(b) obviously "canned" so as to be applicable to every Tom, Dick and Harry who happened to go home to Jesus two days ago; and/or

(c) a whole lot more about the pastor preaching it than about the person who died. I've been to some funerals where I never heard a single identifying characteristic of the person whose life is being celebrated.

The preceding complaints are not just my personalized dislikes. These tend to make the pastor look like s/he is lazy, incompetent, narcissistic, and/or uncaring. And the problem is that the pastor here is *the Vicar of Christ*, and Jesus doesn't appreciate being seen as any of those things.

It *is* my *personal preference* to always use a manuscript for the homily and for the whole liturgy of the funeral. And I make complete transcript booklets of the whole worship on good quality paper, which I give to the family after the funeral is over (trying to make enough copies so that every significant family member gets their own copy.) The reason is that quite often the family "checks out" during the funeral – doing their own personal grief / closure processing. They are "on autopilot." I don't give them the manuscript so they can later say, "Oh, my, what an erudite pastor we have!" I do it, because over and over and over, I have family members tell me how much it has helped in their grief processing to be able to go back and read once more the words of remembrance of their loved one and the words of comfort of the One Who Loves them more than they had ever asked or imagined.

The theology for funerals is pretty basic:

➢ God loves us
➢ God is a merciful God
➢ God is true to the Promises God made, and enacted through Jesus, Who is our very best friend
➢ God has blessed us with this person's unique life, and we are thankful
➢ *Ashes to ashes, dust to dust; if God doesn't get them, the devil must.*

In other words, we *must* respect the fact that none of us knows what goes on either behind closed doors or within the recesses of anyone's heart. None of us knows the story out of which anyone's life has been born. Pastors at a funeral are no more entitled to eat of the Tree of Judgment, than were Adam and Eve! That's God's job. It doesn't matter what your evangelical or social or whatever theological bent may be; *it's God's call, and for you to pass judgment is heresy.* Don't do it.

I pass along one penultimate bit of advice – no, *admonition* -- from the dear saint who taught me how to do funerals in my licensing school: *You are not good enough to torment any family by making them sit in that funeral home or church for more than half an hour. If you do that, I will come back and haunt you myself.*

And the final advice – from the same source: if the family offers to pay you for doing the funeral, do *not* ever refuse it. That's also part of their grief processing. Never ask for a fee for a funeral; never turn down a family's effort to thank you. They're honoring their loved one's memory; your refusal cheapens it, in their mind.

A Nugget

DON'T BE SURPRISED WHEN THE REALLY IMPORTANT ISSUE ONLY POPS UP NEAR THE END OF THE SCHEDULED TIME TOGETHER.

It happens this way, too, with psychological counselors and psychiatrists.

Don't be surprised.

And don't let it cross boundaries you otherwise wouldn't.

It is what it is. Pray about it. Ask yourself and the person who "popped" up this bombshell at the last minute, "I wonder why you brought this up now when our time together is nearly concluded. We'll pick up here next time, and maybe, we can start with why you think it came up this way."

13
Dirty Harry Theology

A person's got to know their limitations.

It was the second in a series of five motion pictures, based on largely gratuitous violence. When *Dirty Harry* in *Magnum Force* was released in 1973, there was a different sensitivity to inclusive language, and "the" line of the movie, with which Lt. Neil Briggs (Hal Holbrook) always badgered Inspector Harry Callahan (Clint Eastwood) was, "A man's got to know his limitations." It was, at the end, the last line that Callahan uttered over the fallen Briggs.

I don't in any way endorse the violent tendencies of that whole movie genre, but the line – even back then – always stuck with me as being very good advice. And it surely is for the pastoral caregiver.

It is gratifying to see how the academy is changing in its perception and teaching of pastoral caregiving, just in the past decade or so. For far too long, although the academic advisory was always given: "A person's got to know their limitations," the academy taught pastoral caregiving in something that looked remarkably like "psychological counseling *light*." The training of pastors today has taken a serious turn toward a different identity – that of spiritual direction.

Pastors are *not* by training, nor identity, equipped to do psychological counseling. Even if they have a background in psychology prior to coming to pastoral ministry (adequate to cover the training deficiency) that is still not our identity. Pastors are Doctors of the Soul. And we need to know the limitations of that. (If for no other reason, there are *enormous liability issues* involved, which are most likely going to be excluded from the insurance policy that your Church carries.)

There is nothing wrong with, and I have found it beneficial to the parishioner on the occasions when I did it, to do spiritual counseling at the same time that the parishioner also seeks mental health counseling from a certified therapist. I have even (at the mental health professional's request) sat in on one of the therapy sessions, so that we could both see how our working with the parishioner / client dovetailed.

It is clear that there is a very strong (and sometimes confusingly imperceptible) overlap between issues of the soul and of the mind. Call it an "emotional" issue, and it makes it even more confusing.

Whatever you call it, if the parishioner is evidencing delusional thinking, a failure to grasp reality, or a danger to self (in this world, as opposed to their eternal future) or others, then you *absolutely must know your limitations. You must refer the parishioner for additional treatment.*

There are a variety of temptations that cause pastors to fail to do so. They include, but are not limited to

(a) a lack of touch with reality – of the pastor (failure to know their own limitations); or

(b) a parishioner who came to you not because it was a "soul condition" but a mental condition, and they could not afford a private secular counselor, and you are just trying to "be nice;" or

(c) a discovery of deeper problems once you began spiritual direction, that you hadn't recognized, and you simply don't know how to "break the news" to the person.

Here's a good "rule of thumb" (although not *always* applicable, though I know some pastors whose denomination now enforces this rigidly): If you can't make progress after three sessions, then you need to make a referral.

An ancillary benefit to this rule-of-thumb is also to recognize your time limits. There are a lot of hurting people in the world. You are the pastor to a whole flock. While crises (hospitalization, death, grief, loss of employment stress, etc.) arise that surely cause us to appropriately spend disproportionate amounts of time with a single person (or very limited number), long term commitments to a very few people in the flock will surely deprive other needy people from receiving the pastoral care that they also need.

Recognition of your limitations is not just in terms of spiritual versus clearly mental health issues. If you have not had specific training in family dynamics counseling (and that doesn't mean a single course in seminary that analyzes "family dynamics" as applicable to the life of the church) then you should not engage in doing it. Your failure to recognize your limitations is not helping these people that you are trying to help. Your delusions of grandeur (and harsh as that may sound, it is accurate) are giving these people false hope. It's not fair to them; it's certainly not fair to your church.

There is a similar issue that will arise (with surprising frequency) to various degrees. It's called *the Messiah complex*. It is a far more common affliction of the congregation than it is of the pastor.[21]

In its most benign form, a member of the flock is so enamored with the compassion, skill, and/or charisma of the pastor, that s/he thinks that there's nothing their pastor cannot do. Sometimes pastors (who have not yet discovered that their self-worth is not dependent upon the valuation done by the flock) will even "feed" this. In such case, the *Dirty Harry Theology* gets lost and the pastor can agree to attempt to do all kinds of things that they are not able to do (ranging from inappropriate counseling through various stages of workaholism, to much worse.)

The much worse scenario is when the pastor becomes the object of a romantic interest of the parishioner. This does not have to be anything that the pastor (knowingly) has encouraged. It's a dynamic that runs along some version of

---

[21] Unfortunately, it *does* occasionally inflict a pastor, who rarely is able to see it her/himself. Peer covenant groups are the best defense against this.

this scenario: the person seeking pastoral counseling feels vulnerable or threatened or unloved or unlovable, etc. The person also often has a history of not receiving what they think is appropriate attention from significant people in their lives. Then, through the intensive, skillful work of the pastoral counselor, they are introduced to the overwhelmingly unconditional love of God through Jesus Christ.

It's the *Vicar of Christ* run amok. They can't see Jesus. They see you. They feel love, and they are looking at you. They make the wrong connection.

I remember the first time this happened to me, as a rookie pastor. I was grateful that the woman was candid about it (as I may not have seen it coming for some time.) It was near the end of a meeting (not even a counseling session, just a church planning meeting.) The woman wanted me to know how much she really appreciated what I was doing in her life. I said something benign (and unsuspecting) like "You're welcome." And she said, "No, I don't think you understand what I'm saying. I really appreciate the difference in my life since I started working with you, and I think that you should know that I am developing feelings for you – romantic feelings. You need to know that."

Like I said, I was *very* appreciative for her candor, because I had not seen this at all!

I am also *even more grateful and appreciative of the quick response on-call work of the Holy Spirit* in that moment. For it took no longer than for me to swallow deeply, and silently groan, "Oh, God! Help me!" than my lips began to speak words that I had no conscious thought of forming:

"Oh, gosh. Geez, we've got an identity issue going on here. You see, since we have been working together, I have been able to see just how much Jesus has been blooming in your life. It really is visible, you know. And I can certainly understand why this makes you feel good. You can't physically see Jesus; you're just seeing me. And you've made an identification error. I'm sure that once you re-focus your feelings in *that* direction, you are going to see, even more so, how great indeed is His love in your life."

And then – and looking back on it later on, I was also able to see the wisdom of the next line – I followed it up with: "And besides, you know that I am very happily married. You need to make sure you understand that there is absolutely zero chance that any romance would ever happen between us."

It was a combination of pastoral direction (on the identity issue) *and* a very firm, personal, male-to-female: NO!

And I'm grateful to say that my advice was right. She did discover the identity substitution, re-focused her attention, and continued to grow in wonderful ways in her own life, marriage, and the life of the Church.

It doesn't always work out that way.

But it should.

And it must!

There is very little that can cause more harm to a church, many innocent people, the ministry of future pastors, and the very Body of Christ – for a very long time – than when a pastor strays, and crosses over boundary lines like this in a Church.

Robert Frost was certainly correct in his poem *Mending Wall*:

"Good fences make good neighbors."

There are boundary lines which, for the sake of the pastor, the flock, and the Body of Christ, absolutely need to be kept.

I am blessed to have a background in the profession of law, which has a very strict Code of Ethics, in which the bright line is *not merely* Don't do the wrong thing, but *more*: *Do not do anything that gives the appearance of impropriety, even if it's not technically wrong*.

Good fences / borders / boundaries are absolutely necessary to effective ministry.

Don't do anything which you would hate to try to explain to your spouse – even if you didn't do anything wrong.

Don't meet with a member of the opposite gender in a counseling situation where anyone can raise an allegation of misconduct. (I have always made it a solid rule that I won't meet with a member of the opposite gender in the Church at any time when no one else is in the building.)

Making sure that no one can raise an allegation against you is a good border to prevent the other person (or <u>you</u>, in a moment of weakness) from being tempted to do something inappropriate.

I learned a technique from working with the State Police that I, at first, thought was a little bit paranoid. I'm come to appreciate it as good sense. Whenever a trooper is transporting a member of the opposite gender, the trooper radios in at the point of departure with their mileage and asks for recordation of the time. Then, as soon as they arrive, the trooper calls back the dispatcher for a recordation of the time and mileage.

Sometimes when you are doing pastoral counseling, you are not dealing with people who are "all together." I remember Potiphar's wife, and am wary against setting myself up for a similar situation (since I have absolutely no desire to either spend time in prison nor to be second in command of the nation of Egypt.) My wife and I even have an understanding, and code, that when I am in a situation in the car where I have any "bleeps on the internal radar in my head" of potential problems, I will call her on my cell phone, and she will note the numbers I give her (interspersed in the verbiage) along with the time of my call. And that gets repeated at the end of the car trip. (It's our version of the State Police protocol.)

There is also the very real actuality of pastors who, invited or not, step over the boundary line on their own.

There is no justification to violate the vows you made to God at your marriage and at your ordination and/or to be a coconspirator in aiding and abetting the violation of the vows the other person made with God at their wedding.

Let me repeat: there is NO justification for it.

And the damage is so devastating for so long. Unless you've gone in and tried to pick up the pieces, one, two, three, and later pastorates removed, you can't begin to fathom how far the ripples from your sinful conduct go.

Is it sexual? For the most part, not. For the most part, pastors who stray are tired and unappreciated, and have been deluded into thinking some momentary fling (usually with someone who suffers from the messiah-projection problem, and who is vulnerable) is something other than what it is.

It happens when pastors are unable to find their worth apart from the adulation of others, and who feel like their tank is near empty.

We are so often telling pastors that they need to attend to self-care issues. Workaholics tend to take this with a grain of salt; it applies to others, not them. They can't see how they are setting themselves up for disaster.

Good fences make good neighbors.

A person's got to know their limitations.

Remember Hallmark: **When you care enough to give your best.** That means you have to take Sabbath, or you can't "give your best" – not to God, not to your family, and not to your flock.

When you don't place boundaries on your schedule, and when you don't provide Sabbath for yourself, you are not only acting hypocritically (as to the clear command from the Lord God, on Whose team you profess to be a team player), but you are denying your flock the best that you can give them.[22]

Are there times when the work of the pastor will run at what seems to be intolerable limits? Yes. Sometimes, stuff happens. And it happens in clusters. That *is* a reality. But, if it is a long term issue, and if you can't take time for Sabbath, you need to seriously look at *Why?* and you need to seriously consider the potential – in many respects.

Eugene Peterson recommends that you use "wide margins" in setting your schedule.[23] By this, he means, leave wide spaces between appointments – room to breathe, room to pray, room to change gears, *and room for things to not go according to plan*. Pastors (particularly compassionate ones, and ones who have a problem saying "no") have a tendency to make schedules based on everything going "just right;" everything happening "according to plan." It almost never does. And they are always running behind, al-

---

[22]   I highly recommend reading, *and following* the book *Sabbath, Restoring the Sacred Rhythm of Rest*, by Wayne Muller (New York: Bantam Books, 1999) I also encourage making "Sabbath keeping" a part of the covenant for your accountable discipleship group.

[23]   *The Contemplative Pastor* (Grand Rapids: W'm B. Eerdmans, 1993)

ways somewhere else when in your presence, and certainly very limited in their ability to be TOTALLY PRESENT.

Once upon a time, there was a rich King – and it must have been back in Old Testament times, because this king had four wives. He loved the fourth wife the most and adorned her with rich robes and treated her to the finest of delicacies. He gave her nothing but the best.

He also loved the third wife very much and was always showing her off to neighboring kingdoms. However, he feared that one day she would leave him for another.

He also loved his second wife. She was his confidant and was always kind, considerate and patient with him. Whenever the King faced a problem, he could confide in her, and she would help him get through the difficult times.

The King's first wife was a very loyal partner and had made great contributions in maintaining his wealth and kingdom. However, he did not love the first wife. Although she loved him deeply, he hardly took notice of her!

One day, the King fell ill and he knew his time was short. He thought of his luxurious life and wondered, "I now have four wives with me, but when I die, I'll be all alone."

Thus, he asked the fourth wife, "I have loved you the most, endowed you with the finest clothing and showered great care over you. Now that I'm dying, will you follow me and keep me company?"

"No way!" replied the fourth wife, and she walked away without another word. Her answer cut like a sharp knife right into his heart.

The sad King then asked the third wife, "I have loved you all my life. Now that I'm dying, will you follow me and keep me company?"

"No!" replied the third wife. "Life is too good! When you die, I'm going to remarry!"

His heart sank and turned cold. He then asked the second wife, "I have always turned to you for help and you've always been there for me. When I die, will you follow me and keep me company?"

"I'm sorry, I can't help you out this time!", replied the second wife. "At the very most, I can only send you to your grave."

146

Her answer came like a bolt of lightning, and the King was devastated.

Then a voice called out: "I'll go with you and follow you no matter where you go." The King looked up, and there was his first wife. She was so skinny as she suffered from malnutrition and neglect. Greatly grieved, the King said "*I SHOULD HAVE TAKEN MUCH BETTER CARE OF YOU WHEN I HAD THE CHANCE!*"

In truth, we all have four spouses in our lives:

Our fourth is our BODY. No matter how much time and effort we lavish in making it look good, it will leave us when we die.

Our third is our POSSESSIONS, STATUS and WEALTH. When we die, it will all go to others.

Our second is our FAMILY and FRIENDS. No matter how much they have been there for us, the furthest they can stay by us is up to the grave.

And our first is our Soul – the one so often neglected in pursuit of wealth, power and pleasures of the world.

However, our Soul is the only thing that will follow us wherever we go. So cultivate, strengthen and cherish it now, for it is the only part of us who will follow us to the throne of God and continue with us throughout Eternity.

You are a Doctor of the Soul. You cannot be a Doctor of anyone's Soul, unless you take care of your own. A person's got to know their limitations. A person's got to take care of the Gift God gave them. Loving your neighbor as yourself, means (among other things) that it's a good thing to include yourself as a neighbor.

Remember the LESSON OF THE AIRLINES. Before each flight takes off, the flight attendant (or a video of a flight attendant) gives an orientation for contingencies on the flight. At one point, each passenger is told:

"In the event of a sudden cabin decompressurization, the panel above your head will open and an oxygen mask will descend." [A demonstration follows of putting it over your mouth and nose, and pulling the two straps at the side, by your ears.]

Next, come those most important words: "*In the event you are traveling with children, or others that need your as-*

sistance, make sure that you put on your mask first, before attempting to assist them."

Even flight attendants understand the theology of Dirty Harry. There's no reason we shouldn't.

A Nugget

One of the powerful Easter images began before the Crucifixion, at the Last Supper, when Jesus told the disciples: "after I am raised up, I will go ahead of you to Galilee." (Matthew 26:32) Then, after the Resurrection, Jesus told Mary Magdalene, and the other Mary: "Do not be afraid; go and tell my brothers to go to Galilee; there they will see me." (Matthew 28:7)

This is the image of the Jesus Who always arrives on the scene before we do, Who is always there first – whether in the confessional, the hospital room, the funeral home, or wherever. To help focus on that, wherever you may be, use this

PRAYER DISCIPLINE

' BE FULLY AWARE OF THIS:

MOMENT. Stop and pay attention to this very moment. NOW is the only time in which we actually live. We can worry about the past or future, but can only live in NOW. Pay attention to it.

LOCATION. Answer the question: "Where am I right now, at this time?" Be specific in describing this place.

EVENT. Describe who and what is present, and what is actually going on in this moment, in this place. Be specific, but without expression of positive or negative judgments.

FEELING. Describe your emotions and feelings in this very moment, in this place, during this event. To the extent that you are able, describe the feelings exhibited by those others persons who share this time, place, and event with you.

JESUS. Be open to sensing His Presence in this moment. Don't limit yourself to preconceived notions. Just allows His Reality and Presence to gradually "appear" to you. Dwell in this, for as long as you can.

14
FREE US FOR JOYFUL OBEDIENCE

Merciful God,
We confess that we have not loved you with
   our whole heart.
We have failed to be an obedient church.
We have not done your will,
We have broken your laws,
We have rebelled against your love,
We have not loved our neighbors, and we
   have not heard the cry of the needy.
Forgive us, we pray.
Free us for joyful obedience,
Through Jesus Christ our Lord. Amen.

"A Service of Word and Table II" (Confession)
United Methodist Hymnal (1989) p. 12

Confession is good for the soul. It really is.

"Spiritual healing is God's work of offering persons balance, harmony, and wholeness of body, mind, spirit, and relationships through **confession**, forgiveness, and reconciliation. Through such healing, God works to bring about reconciliation between God and humanity, among individuals and communities, within each person, and between humanity and the rest of creation" (*This Holy* Mystery, at page 9, quoting *The United Methodist Book of* Worship, at page 613).

In fact, the policy of our Church is that Holy Communion ought never be celebrated without first the making of confession and the receiving of absolution (forgiveness) (*This Holy* Mystery, at page 13)

For like reason, an intentional pastoral caregiver will never offer a pastoral prayer during worship without including a time for the offering of confession of sins, and giving of absolution, if worship is going to be a vehicle of healing.

We are not called to be a "stand in for Jesus" (the "Vicar of Christ") only when we are administering the Blessed Sacraments. I remember, from my CPE experience, the first time I stood at the bedside of a man in the process of dying. It was in Morgantown. This was not going to be an easy death. He had a distressed look on his face; this I knew, although I had never laid eyes on him before. I asked him if he wanted to talk about anything. He looked straight into my eyes – held the gaze for just a few seconds – and then he began without introduction or small talk to make his confession. And when he was finished, I looked straight into his eyes, and without small talk, told him: *In the Name of Jesus Christ, your sins are forgiven.*

And more than just his facial features changed; the whole atmosphere in the room was transformed.

Although I had never seen that child of God before, and never did again, he entrusted me for this most important task – for one simple reason: *"What a shame Jesus Himself is not here, but He sent His Vicar instead."*

What a privilege and responsibility is this call. It is not one for which I have been given the luxury of being off duty, depending upon my mood. I am "on duty" depending upon the need in my presence.

For reasons which I fully confess to not understanding, it is very clear that the Creator hardwired us with a need to confess. This belief was confirmed over and over during my previous career, in my experiences working with police officers. Really good police interrogators are the ones who can mimic a priest or pastor taking confession. Just make the perpetrator think that we know his/her guilt, and can prove it, and therefore it is safe (*i.e.* he will cause himself no further harm) to admit his/her crime, and s/he will spill his/her guts – get it all off his/her chest.

This was true of all but less than a handful of criminals that I worked with as a prosecutor working in the field with his police officers. (I have to admit that one time I was obliged to leave the interrogation room, for risk of messing up the interrogation with laughter, when I was sitting with the fourth suspect that same day who was being told by the same police officer, "Listen, we already know that you did it. We've got all the evidence we need to convict you. I know and you know. Don't you want to just get it off your chest, and come clean.")

I now understand that just as police interrogators increased their effectiveness by modeling a priest or pastor, we pastoral caregivers benefit, too, by learning from those police officer interrogators (not the shucking and jiving part, please!) We need to learn and remember that a critical component is for the person talking to us to <u>feel safe</u> in making their confession.

The parishioner / penitent needs to know that

- ➤ God won't love them any less,
- ➤ I won't love them any less, and
- ➤ I <u>will</u> keep their confession confidential.

As a pastor, I also <u>can</u>not give any appearance, that I know ahead of time what the person needs to confess. I say "<u>can</u>not" instead of "should not" because the cold, hard reality is that, regardless of my suspicions, I really do not know what went on. <u>No one ever knows what goes on behind closed doors</u>. And we certainly cannot <u>know</u> just because someone else told us.

One of my first mentors in ministry told us in Local Pastor Licensing School about his first funeral after graduating from seminary. The dearly departed was the patriarch of not only his church, but of the whole community. He was universally admired and respected throughout the town. The new pastor went to the funeral home, prior to visitation, when he knew that the widow would be there alone. He stood at the back of the room and saw her, alone by the casket, speaking quietly in between what he believed were sobs. He walked closer to provide pastoral comfort. Then he got close enough to hear what she was saying, "Thank God. You'll never beat me again, you S.O.B." That which he had thought were sobs, were really small little laughs. After telling us this vignette, he repeated the lesson: <u>No one ever knows what goes on behind closed doors</u>.

Closely related to this requirement to not pre-conceive what might be the confession, is the absolute prohibition against the pastor expressing any shock. As a prosecutor, I taught a class twice a year to school teachers about dynamics of child abuse and what to do if a child tells them about being abused. The lesson is the same for us: under no circumstances, can you appear to be shocked. For teachers, hearing a small child make a first report of child abuse, any showing of shock could prevent the child from ever again divulging the same, or additional, information. As a pastor, the rationale is pretty much the same. "Shocked" expression can shut down a penitent. Your primary role is to calmly, and with genuine assurance, let them know:

- ➢ God loves them.
- ➢ There is nothing they can do that will change that.
- ➢ There is nothing confessed which God cannot, and will not, forgive.
- ➢ I love them (remember the three rules!)
- ➢ There is nothing they can confess that will change that.

My job as a pastor (indeed the function of every Christian is the same) does not include the function of passing judgment. Remember, what we bind on earth will be bound in heaven, and what we loose on earth will be loosed in heaven. (Matthew 18:18) If our conduct as pastor prevents someone from receiving the blessing and healing of making confession, then we have bound ourselves with their sin.

If we really keep before us, the critical instruction of "Dirty Harry" Callahan (Chapter 13) then we will not only take care of ourselves and carefully observe boundaries, we will also have a very real humility.

And "humility" – properly understood – is not mere false modesty. "Humility" – properly understood – means nothing more nor less than a <u>true</u> self-evaluation.

The medieval Christian classic, *The Cloud of Unknowing,* defines humility thusly: *In itself, humility is nothing else but a [person's] true understanding and awareness of [themself] as [s/he] really is.*

John Wesley give a very similar definition: *a right judgment of ourselves* [Sermons On Several Occasions 17, Par. I.2,]

The attitude of humility is essentially an acceptance of Truth.

Humility is in some respects the <u>master virtue</u> that includes all others. It is knowing that we are all beloved children of God, precious and beautiful to behold – and, furthermore, <u>that the worth</u> of each person <u>comes from God</u> and <u>not from ourselves.</u>

A HUMBLE PERSON is someone who, on one hand, is able to accept responsibility towards others for what s/he does wrong without feeling humiliated by it; and, on the other, is able to accept praise or thanks without feeling particularly embarrassed or a need to lord it over others because of their accomplishments.

Likewise, because a humble person is realistic about all human vulnerabilities, s/he is not unduly shocked or disillusioned when other humans make even terrible mistakes. When it comes to living together, humility is the opposite of perfectionism.

For us pastors to keep this humble spirit, *JUST LIKE OUR PARISHIONERS, WE NEED TO MAKE OUR OWN CONFESSION.* And we need to do so regularly, if we are going to be freed from all our own demons; if we are going to be Freed for Joyful Obedience.

> ➤ We need to make our own confessions, regularly, with a group of trusted spiritual friends.[24]
> ➤ We also need to remember our call.

---

[24] Every pastor absolutely needs to be in some covenant accountable discipleship group. Space here prohibits full discussion of how this works, and reference is made to David Lowes Watson's excellent book, *Covenant Discipleship, Christian Formation through Mutual Accountability* (Nashville: Discipleship Resources, 1994).

> ➤ And we need to keep an eye (by faith) on how it's going to end.

If you haven't been in pastoral ministry long enough to begin to feel the pressures and frustration well up inside you – from the work load, from the uncertain hours, from the inability to regularly see the fruit of seeds planted and nurture given, from the various temptations, and, perhaps, most of all, from the immense weight of carrying, in confidence, the most intense pains and sorrows of people whom we have come to love – then, be patient. It's coming.

Perhaps, we can learn from Mr. Holland about remembering our call, and keeping an eye on how it's going to end. If you had seen only the end of the movie, *Mr. Holland's Opus*, it would be easy to see how Richard Dreyfus' character must have lived a satisfying life. Here were all these people giving testimony to what a difference he had made in their lives.

But, if you remember the rest of the movie, before that satisfying ending, you remembered seeing a frustrated musician, who taught school only as a way to support his family while he went about writing his great symphony. And you remembered the frustrations he faced day and week and month and year, in and out:

> ➤ Students who didn't seem to "get it."
> ➤ A son who was born deaf, so he couldn't appreciate the symphony, even if his father would ever be able to write it.
> ➤ Finally, the doing away with the music department at Mr. Holland's school, which forced his retirement.
> ➤ And, of course, that symphony which never materialized … at least not as Mr. Holland had anticipated.

But the symphony, he finally realized, was the lives of the students.

Perhaps this is a lot like what God's Call is for us.

We'd love to have a musical score before us. We'd like to be able to anticipate the next measure. We'd love to know when it is that we can crescendo into a great movement in our life.

But that's not how it works very often.

156

Isaac didn't have a pleasantly memorable life. After being almost killed as a child by his own father, he got married and had these twin sons, one of whom didn't have a lot of ambition and the other one who was, well, just as lacking in ethics. He grew old, got fooled, and then he died, with his only sons separated by anger and fear.

And yet, because of his faithfulness, and his carrying on the tradition – being the link from the Abraham generation to the Jacob/Israel generation -- the expression we always hear, read, and say is: *the "God of Abraham, Isaac, and Jacob."* The word of his life did not fall to the ground. (cf. 1 Samuel 3:19)

I'm absolutely certain that there were many days and lonely nights when Dr. Martin Luther King, Jr. felt that his words and his actions were simply falling to the ground. But now, every state in this nation celebrates his birthday as a holiday – the only national holiday not based on some military or political career or venture. The word of his life did not fall to the ground.

As the Vicar of Christ, we are called to be faithful. God is the One Who controls whether or not our words fall to the ground.

We may not see the results of the words we use – or the lives that we lead. Indeed there may be times where it seems like the perennial fights over the use of the kitchen, the kind of music being played and sung (or who gets to pick it), and the other prickly bush business of the local and district and conference church are all for naught.

But remember, you were CALLED. And I was CALLED. And at that time, we had an insurmountable compulsion and reason to say: *"Speak, O Lord, for Your servant is listening,"* and to say *"Behold the servant of the Lord; let it be done unto me according to Your Word."*

I can't manufacture for myself a *"George Bailey"* vision like in the movie *"It's a Wonderful Life,"* nor can I see ahead to the final symphony like in *"Mr. Holland's Opus."* But I have heard the words that are spoken each year by our Bishop and the whole flock at Annual Conference to those pastors who are retiring:

> Brothers and sisters in Christ, you came to us from congregations where the Spirit of the Lord was upon

you; and you were charged to preach to the broken-hearted, to visit the captive, to anoint those who were bruised. These things you have done.

We thank God for the community of the faithful in which the Word of God found response. Count-less persons have depended on you for help. In the providence of God, you know that both suffering and joy can be God's way of teaching and healing.

At your ordination, you received authority to read the Holy Scriptures in the church of God, to preach the Word, to celebrate the Sacraments, and to Order the life of the Church. By God's grace you did many things that seemed to be beyond your power.

We thank God that you were given the vision to be faithful. Death and illness have not come on schedule. The truth has not always been easy to preach. We know something of the grace by which you have lived, and we thank God for your vision.

Never think lightly of the great good that God has wrought through you. Continue to be true to your call-ing. May God's love and power be with you always.

God of grace, you fill your servants with the vi-sion. You empower your servants with your Spirit. We give thanks for the ministry of these women and men, and for the ways in which you have ministered through them. Give them a sense of your abiding presence, that they may continue to love and serve you, and ever grow in the grace and knowledge of Jesus Christ, in whose name we pray. AMEN.

And with those words I remember

What

and

Why:

"Speak, O Lord, for Your servant is listening." "Behold the servant of the Lord; let it be done unto me according to Your Word."

> ➢ We need to make our own confessions, regularly, with a group of trusted spiritual friends.
> ➢ We also need to remember our call.

> And we need to keep an eye (by faith) on how it's going to end.

You and I have each received an awesome call, an incredible responsibility, and a power that is more than we can ask or even imagine. Thanks be to God. I leave you with this Native American Blessing:

May the Lord disturb you and trouble you,
May the Lord set an impossible task before you,
And dare you to meet it.
May the Lord give you strength to do your best
And then – but only then –
May you be granted the Lord's Peace.

... and ... FREE YOU FOR JOYFUL OBEDIENCE.

So be it. Shalom.

REMEMBER:

IT TAKES A

WHOLE

LIFETIME

TO PREPARE

A SOUL

FOR

ETERNITY

Made in the USA
Lexington, KY
10 February 2017